Men of Purpose

MEN of PURPOSE
Peter Masters

THE WAKEMAN TRUST ✳ LONDON

© 1973 Peter Masters
1st edition 1973
2nd edition 1975
This revised edition 1989

ISBN 1 870855 04 3

Cover design by Andrew Sides

Printed in Great Britain for The Wakeman Trust, Elephant & Castle, London SE1 6SD, by J. W. Arrowsmith, Bristol, England.

Contents

Acknowledgements

In the original preparation of these biographical sketches in the late 1960s the author was indebted to the facilities of the British Library (then the British Museum Library). For this revised edition considerable gratitude is owed to colleagues at the Metropolitan Tabernacle who processed the revised text and proofs.

Special thanks are due to the following organisations for their courtesy and help in the provision of pictures: H.J.Heinz & Co Ltd for all pictures relating to Henry Heinz; the Cavendish Laboratory of the University of Cambridge for those relating to James Clerk Maxwell; The Royal College of Music for that of Felix Mendelssohn; Warner Pathé Ltd for the Leningrad ballroom; the London Borough of Tower Hamlets for all relating to Fred Charrington; Sheffield City Libraries for all relating to James Montgomery; the Marconi Company for those of the Poldhu transmitting station; University College, London, for that of Fleming as a young man; and the London Borough of Hackney for those of Daniel Defoe's house and pillory.

Thanks are also due to the following professional picture sources: The Science Museum, London, (pages 11, 16, 19, 69, 107, 111, 134 and 140); the National Portrait Gallery (pages 146 and 155); and The Novosti Press Agency (page 58).

The Dawn of Electricity
Michael Faraday

'VERY FEW MEN,' said the scientific writer Sir William Bragg, 'have changed the face of the world as Faraday has done. He was one of the greatest experimental philosophers that ever appeared in this country, or indeed in all the world, and of his discoveries none has had more consequences than that which he made in 1831 ... on this has been founded all those applications of electricity which form the muscles and nerves of our modern life.' Or, as another writer put it, 'The whole world of electricity started with a simple experiment carried out in the Royal Institution by one of the greatest scientists of all times.'

Michael Faraday, extraordinary scientific genius as he became, had a very humble start in life. His father was a village blacksmith in the north of England who migrated to London in search of a living wage. Michael was the third child in the family and was born in rented rooms in London's Elephant and Castle district in 1791. He grew up in an overcrowded home above a coach-house, receiving the slenderest education, and spending most of his early boyhood playing in the street. During years of grave economic recession — particularly the corn shortage of 1800 —

the family lived on Poor Relief, amounting to one small loaf of bread every week for each person.

Yet the Faraday family was a happy family, sharing a faith which meant a great deal to them all. Michael's great grandfather had been noted in village records as a 'stonemason, tiler and separatist', the latter referring to his membership of an independent chapel. His descendants had continued as enthusiastic and dedicated chapel-goers. Young Michael Faraday never missed a Sunday at such a chapel in St Paul's Alley, the City of London, where a small congregation of Christians held firmly to the Bible as the infallible Word of God. Here Faraday learned from the lips of lay preachers a faith which shaped his life and became for him the most important message in the world.

He was thirteen years of age when he took a job as a newspaper and book delivery boy. As he tramped the cobbled streets of early nineteenth-century London, clad in his elder brother's shabby overcoat, he decided to get work as a stationer and bookbinder. But once he became apprenticed another influence intervened. His inquisitive mind would explore the scores of books which passed across his binder's table. Fascinated, he ploughed through Isaac Watts' book *On the Mind*, and began to hunger after a better education. He absorbed complete sections of the *Encyclopaedia Britannica* while rebinding a worn 'E to F' volume, returning again and again to the article on electricity. In his spare time at home he tried to imitate experiments described in the article, and began to track down every popular book or magazine he heard of which contained anything about this fascinating new science.

By now Faraday's brothers and sisters viewed him with a mixture of awe and amusement. It seemed very

Michael Faraday

strange to them that a member of *their* backstreet family should be reading those weighty volumes, paying a shilling a time to attend scientific lectures, and carrying out peculiar experiments with wire and chemicals. They certainly thought he was in a dream world when he began to look for an opening in the world of science. This was how Faraday remembered it:

'When I was a bookseller's apprentice I became very fond of experiments and very adverse to my trade. It so happened that a gentleman, a member of the Royal Institution, took me to hear some of Sir Humphrey Davy's last lectures in Albemarle Street. I took notes and afterwards wrote them out more fairly in a quarto volume. My desire to escape from trade, which I thought vicious and selfish, and to enter into the service of science, which I imagined made its pursuers amiable and liberal, induced me at last to take the bold and simple step of writing to Sir Humphrey Davy.'

The letter to Sir Humphrey enclosed the leather-bound book of beautifully-written lecture notes and asked with youthful optimism if there was any chance of a laboratory job. The reply was non-committal, but not for long, because Sir Humphrey suddenly had to dismiss a laboratory assistant. Then he remembered the young man Faraday, his letter and his nicely written book of lectures.

One evening Faraday was at home undressing for bed when there came a sharp knock at the door. Peering out of his bedroom window he saw an elegant carriage, and a footman holding a letter. It was the letter he had dreamed about — Sir Humphrey inviting him to attend an interview. That interview marked the beginning of Faraday's spectacular scientific career.

He was appointed as a residential laboratory assistant at the Royal Institution, with a modest salary and two rooms at the top of the house.

Faraday had been brought up to believe that people, though capable of many good things, are basically corrupt and sinful. He accepted the explanation of this given in the Bible, that the human race had rebelled against its Maker, and become cut off from Him. Faraday believed that people could only be reconciled to God by seeking His forgiveness, and by trusting in the Saviour Who paid the penalty of sin for all those who love Him. Faraday also believed in the necessity of a personal life-changing conversion. These beliefs had been his faith through youth. But by the time he was twenty-two he was suffering from many doubts. Once he came under the spell of Sir Humphrey Davy, the doubts gave way to open disbelief. Surely, he thought, Sir Humphrey was living evidence that a man could be good and great without believing in Christ.

Sir Humphrey was the idol of the nation. He was a brilliant scientist, an all-surpassing lecturer, and at the same time he seemed to be a model of courtesy, generosity and kindness. Yet *he* was not a Christian. It seemed, after all, that science as well as Christianity could give her devotees qualities of mind and character. But Faraday did not find himself doubting the biblical teaching of man's corrupt nature for long, because the closer he got to his 'model' man, the less he liked the look of him. For eighteen months, as Sir Humphrey's personal assistant, he travelled with him on a grand tour of Europe.

When he returned, he still possessed a great respect for Sir Humphrey as a scientist, but he had little enthusiasm about his qualities or depth of character as a person. Throughout the journey the great man had been very ill-tempered, rash, conceited, unfair and unkind. Faraday returned gratefully to the warm hearts of his family circle and the wisdom of the humble, kindly elders at the old, familiar chapel.

Back at the Royal Institution Faraday now extended his own scientific education by the most formidable programme of reading. But he did not forget his family and would go without dinner every other day in order to pay for his younger sister's schooling. He began to give lectures, and worked solidly on experiments for Sir Humphrey. As the years passed, leading scientists began to realise that the quiet, steady worker in Davy's shadow was no ordinary assistant, and by the time he was nearly thirty, he had made many important discoveries (including that of benzene) and his reputation was growing rapidly.

Without any doubt the greatest attribute of Faraday as a scientist was that he was a *thinker*. His mentor, Humphrey Davy, proceeded on flashes of inspiration, dynamic energy and constant experiments, while Faraday sat down, read about a problem, thought about it, thought a little more, experimented, and then thought still further. He preferred to regard himself as a philosopher rather than a pure chemist, and spent his time hunting for explanations rather than seeking to produce impressive phenomena.

When Faraday wanted to marry Sarah Bernard, the twenty-year-old daughter of one of the chapel elders, she told him that she was rather frightened of 'a mind with a man attached'. However, they entered into one of the most blissful marriages ever recorded in the annals of famous couples. To the day of his death forty-seven years after their marriage they were firmly bound in a tie of understanding, devotion and affection, rarely seen.

It was one month after the happy day of marriage that Faraday publicly nailed his Christian colours to the mast by openly testifying of his faith before his chapel congregation and seeking full church membership. He told the congregation how he had asked the Lord to forgive all his sin, and had yielded over his life to Him. He told them how sure he was that God had heard his prayer, changed his heart, and made him a true Christian. From boyhood he had been an earnest member of the congregation, but not until the age of thirty, when he had passed through his troubled sea of doubts and proved the reality of Christ for himself, did he take this step of joining the church.

Within three years of his marriage Faraday embarked on the great quest for usable electrical power without batteries. Working in his lofty, shelf-lined laboratory at the Royal Institution he made countless experiments with magnets to find the explanation for 'electrical phenomena'. Having been elected a fellow of the Royal Society — despite surprising and petty opposition from Sir Humphrey — he was now in the very forefront of electrical research. When Sir Humphrey died, an unhindered Faraday took complete control of the research activities of the Royal Institution.

In those days electric currents were made in the laboratory by the use of unsophisticated machines which rubbed plates together, or by expensive, cumbersome batteries. Then — in the year 1831 — came Faraday's great discovery. It started with an iron ring six inches in diameter, wound with two, separated coils of wire. The idea was to find whether, if one coil was connected to a battery so that a current flowed

Faraday's 1831 magnet and disc experiment

round it, the separate, unconnected coil would pick up the current. Would the 'live' wire influence the 'dead' wire so as to produce in it a flow of electricity?

The result of this experiment was highly frustrating for Faraday. It worked, and yet it didn't work. It succeeded just enough to tell him that he was on the right path, but it fell so far short of success as to make him realise how much more he needed to discover. In ten days of experimentation and intense thought he secured complete success in making the first real dynamo. He had achieved the production of electricity without a battery, and so laid the foundation stone of the present electronic age. The thinker had uncovered what others had missed by applying his mind to *the space around the magnet* and so grasping the possibility of the existence of a magnetic field and lines of force. This was what led him step by step to his historic dynamo.

Not surprisingly Faraday, at forty-four, was recognised by all as the leading man of science, honoured with a doctorate by Oxford University, and granted a generous government allowance to assist him in his work. Yet personally, he earned no more than the somewhat inadequate salary paid by the Royal Institution, having given up the potential fortune he might have earned from private consultations in order to devote himself to research. The hard-headed businessmen of the day could not understand him. Undoubtedly he was the greatest scientist of the day, and yet how disinterested in the trappings of a wealthy life. A man with his abilities should surely have exploited the discovery of power by making a vast amount of money out of *useful* inventions. Instead Faraday wasted his time playing with wires and magnets!

'What's the use of it?' they would ask tauntingly, as they gathered round the lecturing table after Faraday had finished a public demonstration of some new experiment. 'What's the use of a baby?' was his stock reply. 'Some day it will grow up.' On one occasion the Chancellor of the Exchequer was given a conducted tour of the Institute laboratories, ending with a demonstration of a classic electrical experiment.

Inevitably, the question was asked, 'But Faraday, my dear fellow, what's the use of it?' Immediately the scientist gave his famous reply — 'Sir, there is every probability that you'll soon be able to tax it.'

In 1846 Faraday conceived an understanding of the nature of light far ahead of his time. It was later taken up by James Clerk Maxwell, and later still by Albert Einstein. Out of his great genius and foresight Faraday wrote: 'The view which I am so bold to put forth considers radiation as a high species of vibration in the lines of force which are known to connect particles, and also masses of matter . . . '

Faraday had little interest in the antics of fashionable society. His personal life was centred around his chapel and his family. The chapel building in St Paul's Alley was a typical nonconformist 'preaching box'. It was a plain, wide building with a heavy timber pulpit standing high against the end wall, and a gallery running round the sides and the back. The twenty or so families that formed the membership elected Faraday as an elder when he was nearly fifty years of age. Every week with unfailing regularity he preached at the chapel from notes written on a small white card. Often scientific friends would go along to see what it was that Faraday believed which made him the best-loved man in his profession.

One visitor recorded his impression. 'He read a long portion of one of the Gospels, slowly, reverently, and with such an intelligent and sympathising appreciation of the meaning that I thought I had never before heard as excellent a reader.' Another said that Faraday's object seemed to be to make the most of the words of Scripture, and that his sermons reflected a thorough knowledge of the Bible, for he quoted extensively and accurately. At times his sermons were

Faraday in later life

almost a 'mosaic patchwork of quotes'.

'Throughout his life,' said fellow-scientist Lord Kelvin, 'Faraday adhered faithfully to his faith. I well remember at meetings of the British Association in Aberdeen and Glasgow how he sought out the meeting places of his church.'

Faraday cannot be thought of without reference to his remarkable programme of public lectures at the Royal Institution. He was renowned for his vivid

Faraday lecturing before the Prince Consort at the Royal Institution

illustrations, expression, gestures and humour, all of which combined to give lectures described by a reviewer as — 'deep entertainment as well as profound instruction.' Little wonder the Prince Consort was often present with his two boys, Prince Albert and Prince Edward. Even more entertaining were Faraday's famous Juvenile Lectures held every Christmas when children would at one moment be held entranced by a serious demonstration, and the next, thrown into fits of laughter by some antic of scientific slap-stick. The man who always retained a streak of boyishness was never more at home than among the young people at these lectures.

It was said that if you were Faraday's friend — you had a friend indeed. If you were in his family circle, you were in his sight, his care, his concern and his daily prayers. If you were in his company you were in the presence of a 'moral tonic'.

Faraday's most significant lectures were often adorned by a reference to the Christian faith. Lecturing before the Prince Consort in 1854, Faraday uttered these words: 'High as man is placed above the creatures around him, there is a higher and far more exalted position within his view, and the ways are infinite in which he occupies his thoughts about the fears, hopes or expectations about a future life. I believe that the truth of that future cannot be brought to his knowledge by an exertion of his mental powers however exalted they may be. It is made known to him by a teaching other than his own, and is received through simple belief of the testimony given. Let no one suppose for a moment that the self-education I am about to commend in respect of the things of this life extends to any consideration of the hope set before us, as if any by reasoning could find out God.'

Faraday had found an understanding of life's purpose by studying and believing the teaching of the
Bible, and by seeking a personal experience of the
Lord Jesus Christ. The gateway to that experience had
been the realisation of his sinfulness before God, and
the need to repent of his sins and surrender his life to
God. 'Without the conviction of sin,' he said, 'there is
no ground of hope to the Christian.'

In the closing years of his life he was granted by
Queen Victoria a stately 'grace and favour' residence
at Hampton Court. There, as the end drew near, he
wrote: 'My worldly faculties are slipping away day by
day. Happy it is for all of us that the true good does
not lie in them. As they ebb, may they leave us as little
children, trusting in the Father of mercies and accep-
ting His unspeakable gift. I bow before Him Who is
Lord of all.'

Faraday died in 1867 at Hampton Court. At his
death he held no less than ninety-seven distinctions
from international academies of science — all of them
unsought. How significant it is that not only Faraday
— the *thinking* scientist — but some of the principal
figures who were to follow him in constructing the
electrical age, were earnest believers in the same
message of salvation. Clerk Maxwell, Lord Kelvin and
Sir John Ambrose Fleming — all held tenaciously to
the same beliefs, and all spoke humbly of having
experienced the great change of a personal conversion
to God.

Founder of a Food Empire
Henry J. Heinz

SIX MILES UP THE Allegheny River, east of Pittsburgh, Pennsylvania, the littler frontier village of Sharpsburg looked out across miles of prairie. To an eight-year-old boy growing up in the mid-nineteenth century the prairie, with its buffalo herds and painted Indian warriors, seemed to be the rest of the world. True, he had heard of the other great states of America, the ever-expanding cities, the huge factories and the advancing railroads, but where he lived the stagecoach was the only organised link with the rest of civilisation, and the village did not even have a morse-telegraph station.

This was the world of Henry J. Heinz — the eldest boy of a family of German immigrants. Sharpsburg, in its isolation, was a place which demanded great humour and resourcefulness from its few hundred inhabitants. Every morning young Heinz would make his way up the mud road to school, where one large class was taught by a warm-hearted, dedicated Lutheran pastor. Every afternoon, back at home, he worked like a Trojan in his mother's rambling kitchen garden, which supplied almost everything the household ate. After that, his final chore was to tour the

The Heinz home at Sharpsburg

village selling their surplus vegetables from a basket.

As he lived out the spartan routine of his boyhood, Henry Heinz looked in his imagination far beyond the horizons of the prairie — beyond even the unseen wonders of the industrial cities with their increasing mechanisation. He would think often about an amazing Person — Jesus Christ — Who once walked an Eastern prairie, a land of camels, palm trees and Roman soldiers. He regarded Him, as did his mother and the Lutheran pastor, as the Son of God; the Lord of Glory. Young Heinz understood the meaning of that awesome day when the Lord allowed Himself to be nailed to a wooden cross to die in agony. 'My sins,' he thought, 'were punished there! He was *my* Saviour, for He died in my place, and the Lord laid on Him the iniquity of us all!'

To Henry Heinz, Jesus Christ was the Lord of Heaven and earth; above and beyond, yet everywhere; in the Heinz household, and in the lives and hearts of his parents. He was a Lord the youngest child could speak to and know; a Lord to be served and obeyed. The Bible was the main textbook at young Henry's school, and Christian living was the great theme of home life. 'In living for the Master and serving Him,' said Heinz in later years, 'some things have been incalculably helpful and I turn with grateful heart to the teaching of my mother. Many of her sayings ever stand guard around my thoughts and influence my actions.'

As the firstborn of their eight children, Henry's parents hoped that he would become a church minister, but he was so successful and indispensable in the garden, and later in the family business, that nothing ever came of it. He was only ten when his gardening activities led to his selling a wheelbarrow-full of vegetables round the village every day, and at twelve he was growing enough to load a horse and cart. Even at this age he could react with speed and effectiveness to adult-sized problems. One season the swirling Allegheny River rose unusually high and washed away part of the family's land. Henry Heinz took a strong old cart-horse some way down river, dredged several tons of gravel from a reach and tipped it into the river by his home to form an embankment. To the surprise of his parents, the rest of the garden was saved.

Schooldays over, the garden flourished to such an extent that it became a small market garden and labourers were needed to tend it. In addition to supervising that, Heinz turned his attention to helping his father with his tiny, struggling brick-making

Henry J. Heinz at the time of his visit to London

business. Bricks never lost their fascination for Heinz. To his dying day he would always pause to admire well-made bricks and handsome brickwork. The wall materials for all his factories were hand-picked, and at the height of his success in the food business his desk drawers would be sure to be crammed with brick samples.

In 1869, when he was twenty-five, he married Sarah Young, also a fervent Christian believer. Together they set out to serve the Lord. 1869 was also the year in which the first 'Henry J. Heinz Food' firm graced the company registers. He took a plot of land, two rooms and a cellar to begin the production of bottled horseradish. The trouble with fresh horseradish was its preparation. Washing and grating it was a worse experience than peeling onions. But Henry Heinz put an end to this painful household chore by turning out bottles of ready-grated horseradish by the thousand. His product was an instant and spectacular success.

While the firm grew — with all its attendant problems — Heinz still found time to run his local Sunday School. He prepared meetings, led the worship of the children, taught, and gave spiritual counsel with an affection which was seldom forgotten by his 'scholars'. At a very crucial time in the expansion of his firm, when all his resources were bent upon the development of new plant, he was deeply challenged within himself about the financial support he gave for Christian work. The church he attended had just erected a new building and still owed a substantial amount of the cost. The church officers — including Heinz — met together, and one of those present suggested that they should each contribute a very large share of the money.

As different officers volunteered their subscriptions

Heinz struggled with his thoughts. He was younger than the others, recently married, and financially committed to a rapidly growing business. He could not afford to pledge away this money, but he remembered the promises he had made to the Lord to shirk no duty and to contribute liberally. He volunteered the money, telling his family afterwards, 'If the Lord wants me to do this, He will help me to make good my pledge.' He learned early in life that his prime responsibility as a Christian was to his Lord's work.

As the years went by the food-bottling company acquired 125 acres of ground and expanded to produce several varieties of product. But trouble lay ahead. The company badly needed extra supplies of vegetables to meet requirements, so they undertook to buy the entire produce of a farm in Illinois. As long as the vegetables were sound, Heinz agreed to take everything. All went well until the United States experienced the most phenomenal harvest ever known. The Illinois farm produced an astounding crop, supplied it to the Heinz factory at Pittsburgh and demanded payment. 2,000 bushels of cucumber alone were culled from the fields in one month, calling for payment of $1,200 a day. And the harvest seemed to go on and on.

In the ordinary way Heinz could easily have secured a bank overdraft to pay for it all, but at this particular time the entire nation was in the middle of an economic catastrophe which was closing hundreds of banks and bringing some of the largest companies into liquidation. No one could get credit anywhere. Heinz poured everything he had into the business and took every possible step to secure extra cash to pay for this relentless flow of vegetables. Somehow he met the demands until, with the freak crop still coming in,

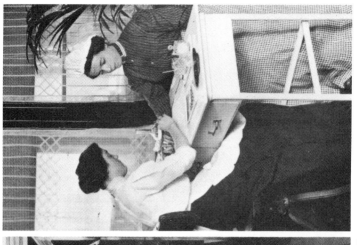

Weekly manicure and fine facilities graced the Heinz factories

he reached the end of his resources and wrote to his mother, 'I fear we shall not be able to pull through the panic...I am afraid that our firm will have to be numbered among the thousands that are falling daily.'

The firm finally fell at Christmas leaving Heinz penniless. But even in the midst of disaster there was a faith and an unswerving integrity about Henry Heinz which stood out in the turbulent world of business. In those hard pioneer townships a man was considered a fool if he did not confine himself to looking after his own skin. But Heinz was determined to honour his promises, and set himself the target of clearing any and every debt arising from the failure of his firm, regardless of the fact that a bankruptcy court discharged him from liability.

In a book labelled, 'M.O.Book' (Moral Obligation Book) he listed everyone to whom the firm had owed money. Not surprisingly, when Heinz's relations pressed him to go back into business with their savings, his own former creditors did everything to help him because they respected and trusted him completely. The landlord of his former business property gave him a new lease free of rent for a time, and the business was off to a fresh start. Once again the small figure of Heinz, bristling with energy could be seen moving here and there in the factory showing someone how something could be done better, encouraging staff and making constant notes about improvements which could be made. In no time at all the small bottles of *Pure Food Products* appeared in the shops once more to mark the beginning of a new and outstanding chapter in the life of the firm.

Heinz was a great character, truly appreciated by his growing body of employees. Supremely he was a man of action, whose slight build disguised a dynamic and resilient character. He wore a huge moustache, carried a permanent twinkle in his eye, and simply radiated energy. A compulsive teacher, he was always ready to give a voluble, demonstrative, and persuasive lesson on almost anything he knew about.

Here was a man of such warmth and feeling that his very presence tended to melt the discontented and spur the dispirited. Ideas, policies and sales methods poured from him in a steady stream, though office routine was virtually non-existent with him. His closest colleagues could not recall that he ever spent more than twenty consecutive minutes in desk work. As he devised new manufacturing processes, evolved sales methods and concocted recipes, the firm saw rapid expansion. Extra land was acquired, new factories erected and an even greater variety of products introduced. Still the 'Heinz ideals' had to be maintained. Premises must be the cleanest anywhere. The buying of raw materials and the selling methods must be absolutely straight and fair.

H.J.Heinz was one of the first American companies to introduce staff welfare facilities. The founder insisted that the firm provided staff with dining rooms, locker rooms, dressing rooms, gymnasia, swimming pools, uniforms, free hospital and dental treatment, free life insurance and further education facilities. The result was that few people ever left the sprawling Heinz empire at Pittsburgh. At the centre of it all, Heinz remained — in the words of one of his executives — 'a monument of inner peace'.

He was forty-two and the head of a nationwide company when he at last gave way to a lifelong urge to travel. Europe was his great goal; England, the home of so many spiritual wonders; and Germany, the land of his parents. In addition he had a great

*Heinz arrives
at Fortnum
and Mason*

ambition to personally introduce Heinz Pure Food Products to London's most celebrated food store — Fortnum and Mason's in Piccadilly.

Heinz embarked for Europe in 1886, accompanied by his wife and four children. He had decided to travel on the *SS City of Berlin*, a very large, bluff-bowed paddle steamer bound for Liverpool. His notebook (which he was seldom without) recorded every detail which caught his eye. The size of the ship, its age, speed, tonnage, crew, history, horsepower, and equipment, were all duly noted. Not much escaped the eagle eye and boyish inquisitiveness of this builder and dreamer. On disembarking, Liverpool got a similar inspection. Out came the rolled metal tape measure which he always carried, and unusual doorways, strange brickwork patterns and architectural novelties were all deftly measured and noted.

Yet clearly the most significant entries in Heinz's travelling notebook are those which show his passion for the spiritual heritage of 'little old England'. Passing through Bedford he filled pages with comments on Bunyan and *The Pilgrim's Progress*. In London, his favourite day of the week gave rise to profuse notes. 'This being Sunday . . . we all drove to the City Road Chapel, the most historic Methodist Church in the world, erected by John Wesley in 1778.' He expresses warm sentiments for John and Charles Wesley and records enthusiastically the history of early Methodism.

Across the road from the chapel in Bunhill Fields he found the tombs of Bunyan, Cromwell and Isaac Watts — names that meant a great deal to him. Sunday afternoon found him sitting in on a Sunday School meeting, comparing and contrasting it with his own Sunday School back at Pittsburgh. Then, in the evening, a carriage took him to hear Charles Haddon Spurgeon preach at the crowded Metropolitan Tabernacle — 'The humblest and simplest great man I have ever heard.'

Fortnum and Mason's (by appointment suppliers of provisions to the Royal Household) presented a great challenge to Heinz who was an instinctive and enthusiastic salesman. One morning armed with five cases of Heinz foods he took a cab and drove to conquer the famous store. Top hat in hand he swept in and crisply secured the attention of a senior member of staff.

The Fortnum and Mason's man stood passive and intent as the small but commanding American with sparkling eyes and large moustache announced himself and produced his pure delicacies from Pittsburgh. Having delivered his opening volley of persuasion Heinz paused, eyes glinting, ready to counter the first defensive objections of the Fortnum and Mason's man. To his partial disappointment, for he loved a battle, a quiet voice murmured, 'Mr Heinz, we will take them all.' Heinz foods had entered the English market. Some years after this first visit to England a permanent London branch was organised with a small warehouse near the Tower of London.

For nearly a century all Heinz products carried the trade mark, '57 varieties', one of the most successful and memorable slogans in the history of marketing. The famous number was Henry Heinz's own idea. One day, travelling in an overhead train in New York, he noticed an advertisement for a brand of shoes which boasted '21 styles'. Turning it over in his mind he thought of his own enormous number of food varieties, and the '57' logo was born.

Heinz visits his harvesters; 1908

Throughout his life he continued to be very active as a Sunday School superintendent, giving very considerable financial support to Sunday School work in numerous churches. For twenty-five years he helped to build up and run a state-wide organisation for the encouragement of Sunday School work and participated in many special campaigns to visit homes and encourage people to attend church. In one special campaign he directed house-to-house visitation in Pittsburgh for which over 2,000 visitors were trained and over 83,000 homes visited. He also sponsored the promotion of Sunday Schools in such far-away places as Japan. In 1918 he led twenty-nine pastors and businessmen through seventy cities of Japan, Korea and China. Constantly he made himself available to visit and address churches on the importance of reaching the rising generation for God through the work of Sunday Schools and youth Bible Classes.

At the time of his death in 1919, Heinz's firm had 6,523 employees, 26 factories, 227 offices and other premises and 100,000 acres of farmland. But when the obituaries were published in the press his own order of priorities in life was fairly reflected — 'Henry J. Heinz, churchman, philanthropist, manufacturer...'

'The real passion of his life,' said the Dean of Pittsburgh University, 'was his religion.' And Henry J. Heinz made it very clear what he meant by religion when he prefaced his Last Will and Testament with these words:–

'Looking forward to the time when my earthly career shall end, I desire to set forth, at the very beginning of this Will, as the most important item in it, a confession of my faith in Jesus Christ as my Saviour.'

A Composer's Journey
Felix Mendelssohn

MOSES MENDELSSOHN turned up in Berlin in a very sorry state. Fourteen years old, he was exhausted and dusty from days of walking. He was emaciated, ugly, deformed, and bore the added stigma for those days of being a Jew. He arrived alone and stood before the guards at the main city gate to seek admission. When asked his business he tried his one solitary word of German. 'Lernen,' he stammered — to learn.

The guards sent him round to the livestock gate, because Jews were denied the use of the main entrance, and there the guardroom register for the day contained the entry: 'Today there passed through the Rosenthaler Gate six oxen, seven swine, one Jew.' That was in 1743. Six years later the 'dark little hunchback' was Berlin's most provocative writer and philosopher, and by 1767 his one word of German had mushroomed into many famous books.

Moses was a creative writer; a thinker of irrepressible genius. His son Abraham (one of eight children) did not seem to be cast in the same mould at all. A large, handsome, slow-moving man, he steadily built a huge bank from a little capital. Rich, staid and conservative he argued with no one and invested other people's fortunes with impregnable reliability. But that flash of fire which had lifted Moses Mendelssohn from obscurity to fame re-emerged in his grandson.

Felix Mendelssohn was born in 1809, the year in which Haydn died and the year before Chopin's birth. Unlike other composers, riches and luxury surrounded Mendelssohn from birth. Only one thing marred the smile of affluence — he was a Jew. His father had worried about this for years because according to the law, if the State wished to be vindictive, all his fortune and properties could be confiscated overnight. As a Jew in Berlin he was entitled to nothing.

Naturally, Abraham Mendelssohn avoided any show of wealth and kept his luxuries behind the facade of a plain-fronted house. He also worried for the sake of his children. Why should they have to endure the scorn and contempt of the race-conscious Berliners of those days?

Abraham Mendelssohn felt no personal loyalty to Judaism for he did not positively believe that God had supernaturally spoken to the Jews and dealt with them as recorded in the Bible. He was therefore readily impressed by the reasoning of his brother, who said: 'A man can only remain loyal to an oppressed, persecuted religion and impose lifelong persecution upon his children so long as he thinks it is the only way of salvation. But as soon as he no longer believes that, it is barbarism for him to do anything of the kind.'

One evening Felix, still a small boy, came home from the singing school crying bitterly. Rushing up to his father with eyes streaming he told him how the other children had taunted him during the singing of the St Matthew Passion. They had chanted, 'Look at the Jew-boy singing to Christ!' On hearing this, his father's deliberations were brought to a head immediately. The very next day he took his children to a Lutheran Church where they were turned into state-recognised Christians with a few drops of baptismal water. The parents sought the protective mantle of Christianity by applying for formal membership of the church soon afterwards.

The wealthy banker's acceptance of Christianity was a purely nominal act as may be seen from letters to his daughter. 'Does God exist?' he asked in one, '...Do we live on? If so, where and how? I do not know the answers to any of these questions and have therefore never taught you anything concerning them.' So while the Mendelssohn children were now brought up as 'Christians' there was no conviction behind it. The family's adopted Protestantism was the kind of colourless, respectable creed which has led countless others to spurn Christianity for the rest of their lives.

Music meant much more to Felix. It seized hold of him at the tender age of six, and by the time he was nine he was ready to make his first public appearance as a pianist. At ten he began composing, producing over fifty complete movements in eighteen months. The most remarkable event of his youth was the extravagant reaction of Germany's top musical connoisseurs when he played before them at the age of twelve.

His elderly tutor, a tall, distinguished musician named Zelter had arranged for him to perform in the presence of Goethe, a Minister of State, and a number of accomplished musicians. Before young Mendelssohn was ushered into Goethe's richly furnished music room, Zelter looked gravely at the eminent company and said, 'I have come in first, gentlemen, to ask you a favour. You are about to meet a twelve-year-old boy whose ability on a piano will astound you, and whose ability for composing will astound you even more. If you are moved to flatter him please do so with moderation and in C major, the most colourless of keys. Up till now I have managed to preserve him from vanity.'

Felix entered the room. He was slightly built with long black hair, and looked young for his age. As soon as he began to play his listeners sat up and leaned forward in their seats. Rapt attention mingled with amazement.

Later the same day, Felix gave another recital before a much larger audience of notables. One of the musicians present described the effect he produced: 'The gentle melody was transformed into a surging figure which he took first in the bass, then in the soprano voice, developing it with lovely contrasts creating a torrential fantasia that poured like liquid fire ... the whole company was thunderstruck ... the boy's small hands worked into masses of tone, mastered the most difficult combinations; the passages rumbled and dropped like so many pearls!' (Rellstab, quoted by Richard and Clara Winston.)

Such was the skill and dexterity of the young Mendelssohn that Moscheles, the renowned pianist, recorded in his diary: 'Felix is a phenomenon. What are all prodigies compared with him? Gifted children — nothing more! This boy is already a mature performer.'

Felix was sixteen when his father decided to buy one of Berlin's finest mansions, enriched by the rare and magnificent luxury of extensive lawns and gardens. Here the friendly, vigorous prodigy surrounded

Mendelssohn with Victoria and Albert

himself with a large company of friends drawn from the affluent youth of the city. They read Shakespeare together (which had just become available in German), formed an orchestra and choir, and centred their leisure lives on the Mendelssohn mansion. Everything was there; every facility to cultivate artistic flair; to walk, talk, argue and joke with the progeny of Prussia's leading families. Never had an emerging composer known such an environment.

It was the magnificent garden of the stately Mendelssohn home that enchanted and overpowered Felix
one hot, August evening, inspiring him to produce his
first successful composition. He sat alone and as a
gentle breeze dispersed the fragrance of shrubs into
the warm night air, and fireflies darted to and fro, the
strains of *A Midsummer Night's Dream* formed in his
mind. 'That night,' he recalled, 'I encountered Shakespeare in that garden.'

There was another 'encounter' earnestly desired by
the sensitive spirit of Mendelssohn. He, like all his
rich young friends, lived for the present. They thrived
on and were motivated by mutual flattery, pride,
pleasures, hopes and aspirations. But what was the
underlying purpose of it all? His family had been
'converted' from Judaism to Christianity, but neither
his father nor his mother believed in the new faith any
more than they had trusted the old. Even the various
theological dignitaries who frequently visited the
house to be entertained by his father seemed to be
more interested in *disproving* Christianity than in
following it. It was becoming fashionable in Germany
to ridicule the divine inspiration and authority of the
Bible.

Perhaps the answer lay in Catholicism. As soon as
Felix had time (he was now a student at the University
of Berlin) he determined to look into the beliefs of
Rome. But before he started his investigation Bach
intervened. The voice of Bach, 'arch-Protestant'
composer of the previous century, could still ring in a
musician's ears.

One of Mendelssohn's friends had remarked that
Bach's music was dry and mechanical, and Felix had
formed a small Bach chorus of sixteen voices to prove
him wrong. He certainly developed a reverential

appreciation of the St Matthew Passion, a work he longed to see performed in Berlin. The year 1829, the hundredth birthday of the work, provided a golden opportunity. With the help of a close friend, the singer Edward Devrient, Felix assembled an orchestra and a choir of 400 for the occasion. When the work was performed — conducted by Felix — it met with resounding acclaim from the people of Berlin.

Mendelssohn's own attachment to it went deeper than the musical and dramatic impact. He had begun to develop a profound respect for the spiritual message of the Passion. It brought him to a literal belief in the sufferings and death of Christ as a substitutionary atonement for man's sin. It brought him to an equally firm belief in the divine inspiration and infallibility of the words of Holy Scripture.

So far as can be ascertained the only acquaintance of Felix's at that time who held similar views was a young man studying at Berlin for the Lutheran ministry. Apart from walking and talking with this friend, Mendelssohn had only the Bible and Bach to help him in his quest. He was searching for the meaning of life in a direction his family and most of his friends scoffed at.

Fresh from the triumphant performances of the St Matthew Passion, Felix made his first trip to London, which he described as 'the grandest and most complicated monster on the face of the earth. Things roll and whirl around me and carry me along as if in a vortex.' His public appearances and travels took him to Wales and Scotland, where the well-known Fingal's Cave incident triggered off the Hebrides overture.

On returning home, it was suggested to him that he compose something to mark the three-hundredth anniversary celebrations of the Lutheran Church's Augsburg Confession. The idea appealed to him and he began to make a study of the life of Luther.

As he read about the spiritual pilgrimage of the Reformer, he was *overwhelmed*. The search for righteousness and acceptance with God that Luther had made was so much more ardent than his own. Luther's failure to find God in a monastery, his ultimate discovery that God makes Himself known to the contrite sinner by faith in Christ, the dramatic experience of his conversion, and his mighty achievements by the clear help of God — all these things buried themselves deeply in Mendelssohn's heart. His feelings found expression in his Reformation Symphony, the most powerful section of which is the paraphrase of Martin Luther's hymn — *A Mighty Fortress is Our God.* Ever afterwards he carried with him for spiritual help and encouragement a copy of Luther's hymns.

When at the age of twenty-one Mendelssohn eventually visited Rome it was no longer to search for truth. He had already come to regard Catholicism as a counterfeit religion devoid of biblical foundation. He was quite interested in the musical aspect of Roman worship but he abhorred the chanting, saying, 'Truly there is in the Bible no basis at all for this monotonous formula. Everything *there* is fresh and true, and the method of expression always as good and fresh as it could possibly be.'

Berlioz met Mendelssohn several times on this Italian trip, recording these sentiments in his diary: 'I firmly believe that M. is one of the greatest capacities of the age ... he is one of those candid souls one so rarely meets. He believes firmly in his Lutheran religion and I scandalise him sometimes by laughing at the Bible.'

Felix Mendelssohn

Felix's reaction to the countless priests, superstition, and religious pomp and ritual of Rome was to
think of his homeland and say, 'Thank God that the
highly-vaunted middle ages are past and can never
return!'

Mendelssohn was a young man of many moods.
The beauties of nature evoked extreme romanticism;
companions stimulated his sense of humour; the
pressures of life stirred a streak of doggedness
inherited from his father; while tragedy or sadness
threw him into the darkness of awful and protracted
depression. Superficiality and escapism he could not
abide. The New Year, for instance, was to him a time
to face up to the failure and inadequacy of the passing
year. It was a time to seek pardon and forgiveness
from Almighty God, otherwise there seemed no point
in making vows and wishing good wishes. 'The way
people meet each other and thoughtlessly, jokingly
wish each other a happy future . . . the way they try to
get rid of the sadness with laughter and drinking, and
cannot do it . . . all this I find absolutely deadly. New
Year days are days of atonement and one should
experience them all alone with oneself.'

With the growing success of his Italian Symphony,
Mendelssohn's fame increased and he was personally
lifted higher and higher in a sense of satisfaction and
well-being. But then he was suddenly plunged into
the most bitter disappointment of his life when the
most prestigious music academy of Berlin rejected
him in the election of a new Director. For all his
searching after God it became apparent to Mendelssohn that he still had far too much at stake in this
world to be able to withstand such a blow to his pride.
Like a stricken deer he left the city of his upbringing
and accepted a post as General Musical Director in

Düsseldorf, becoming deeply involved in the affairs of the theatre.

All these things proved to work together for his spiritual good. His rejection in Berlin taught him not to lay up treasure on earth, and his association with the theatre showed him the corruption and decay which surrounds and engulfs the worldling's 'treasure'. He found in the theatre a totally artificial and morally-decadent world which sickened him, and he just had to break with it.

Mendelssohn may not have had the dramatic experience of the apostle Paul, whose conversion came with a flash of blinding light, but he made the same discovery — that a Christian is a person whom the Lord has made a new creation. 'The old has passed away,' said Paul, and with it all the person's former desires and motives. Felix could readily identify with Paul in this. Small wonder when he published *St Paul* as his first major choral piece, a close friend said, 'The subject chooses us, not us the subject.'

When Mendelssohn began *St Paul* he did not need to think for long about finding a collaborator and adviser for the text. The natural choice was his trusted friend and confidant, the former theological student, who was by now a Lutheran pastor. At first, the pastor hesitated, saying, 'The Lord, in His mercy, gives me liberty and fruitfulness in the work of preaching. I do not think I am really fitted for what you ask.' But Felix wanted to be sure that his theological adviser was a man who believed the old Gospel and who stood by the inspired Word of God. This was his man.

When his father died Mendelssohn found himself more closely than ever identified with the message of the apostle Paul. His last 'earthly prop' had passed away and left him desiring above all else to enter more fully into the new life which he felt God had given him — the life of a converted person. For weeks he was to be seen deeply engrossed in the study of Paul. His Bible, and a volume on early church history, accompanied him everywhere. He was twenty-seven when *St Paul* was first performed, everything about the work reflecting the efforts of an earnest believer concerned both to impart a message and to honour God in the manner of its presentation.

Mendelssohn felt, for example, that the voice of Christ could not be a man's voice, for that might be a transgression of the second commandment. Instead he used a chorus of women's voices to get as far from realism as possible.

The general public, who liked to think of Mendelssohn as a romantic figure, reacted with enthusiasm when at twenty-eight he married Cecile Jeanrenaud, a shy and beautiful girl of seventeen. Cecile, a pastor's daughter, shared his Christian faith and their partnership became one of the famous happy marriages of their century. Why at this stage of his life did he choose to set to music *Psalm 42* — 'As a hart longs for the streams that flow, so does my soul long for Thee, O God!'? Was it because the glamorous circle of young friends of which he had been the centre, openly disdained his religious convictions and ridiculed his evident love of a Saviour? 'My tears have been my food day and night,' says the psalmist, 'while men continually say to me, "Where is your God?" '

Mendelssohn had found that the Christian can be a lonely person in a crowded world. Just as he had found that Paul's experience of conversion had come true in his own life, now he began to understand Elijah, the solitary prophet, whom he chose as the subject for his next major work. Writing to a friend he called Elijah, 'a prophet such as we could use again today — strong, zealous, angry and gloomy in opposition to the leaders, the masses, and indeed the whole world!'

When Frederick William IV had ascended the throne of Prussia one of his first acts was to create a national academy for the arts and persuade Felix Mendelssohn to become its Director of Music. It was in this capacity that the composer was received by Victoria and Albert at Buckingham Palace in 1842. The prince particularly wanted him to spend a Saturday with him to try the organ newly installed in the palace. Mendelssohn was in the course of playing music from *St Paul* when to his surprise both the queen and the prince joined in singing the words. They kept him there singing and playing together long beyond the intended time and left him with one of the queen's personal rings as a token of affection.

Several spiritual compositions and psalms, including the well-known *Hymn of Praise* and the English anthem *Hear my Prayer* came from Mendelssohn's pen before *Elijah* was complete. When the latter finally appeared, it made a tremendous, dramatic impact. But not everyone was happy. Mendelssohn came under heavy fire for his apparent belief in the authority and historical accuracy of the Bible. Both he and his pastoral helper were pilloried for completely ignoring the theories of the liberal theologians. Some critics described the work as, 'A weak potpourri of religious fantasia and sanctimonious preacher's piety.'

Mendelssohn longed to somehow communicate through such choral work a biblical view of the world. When, during his tenth and last visit to England, Sir Julius Benedict asked him what passage of

the Old Testament he most prized, Mendelssohn
picked up a Bible and read: *Vanity of vanities; all is
vanity. What profit hath a man of all his labour which
he taketh under the sun?...All things are full of
labour; man cannot utter it: the eye is not satisfied
with seeing, nor the ear filled with hearing...Is there
anything whereof it may be said, See, this is new?
(Ecclesiastes 1:2-10).* With a sigh the composer asked,
'Who could set that to music?'

During this last visit to England, Mendelssohn was
personally requested by Queen Victoria to conduct
the *Elijah* in London. At the close of the performance
Prince Albert passed him a copy of the programme on
which he had written, 'To the noble artist who,
surrounded by the Baal-worship of debased art has
been able by his genius and science to preserve
faithfully like another Elijah the worship of true art
...to the Great Master Who makes us conscious of
the unity of His conception through the whole magic
of creation...inscribed in grateful remembrance by
Albert.'

That royal appreciation was written in May 1847,
when Mendelssohn was thirty-eight. Six months later
in Leipzig, following a sudden illness, the great
composer true to his own premonition, died an early
death.

The 'Lord Apostol'
Lord Radstock

ONE OF THE GREATEST testimonies to the reality of Christian conversion and the power of the Gospel message is to be found today in the USSR, where thousands of congregations of Christian believers have thrived and grown despite decades of bitter persecution aimed at eradicating faith in God. Not until 1987 did this persecution begin to subside. Yet half-way through the nineteenth century, the light of biblical Christianity had been all but extinguished across the vast land of Russia. The Russian Orthodox Church presented a religion of fear, superstition and ritualism. Gone was the element of spiritual life and fervour which had been present earlier in that century, when even the Tsar professed conversion to Christ. Then, in the 1870s, the flame of true Bible Christianity was rekindled.

How was that flame rekindled? Very largely by a man who was not a church minister or clergyman, nor even a Russian, but an extraordinary English peer who dedicated his life to spreading the Christian faith. He was Lord Radstock, born in 1833 as the Hon Granville Waldegrave. Behind him lay an ancestry of

colourful (often fiery) noblemen going back to
William the Conqueror. Both his father and his
grandfather had been tough, impetuous admirals, and
young Granville seemed to be cast in the self-same
mould.

He grew up a thickset, impulsive boy, who threw
everything he had into life, and dreamed of the status
and power which time would be bound to bring him.
Although his father and mother impressed upon him
the vital importance of seeking a real relationship with
God, the future peer pushed all such ideas into the
background and said to himself, 'Only just so much
of the religious life need be added to this earthly life.'

Away at Harrow School, and later at Balliol College, Oxford, he followed the typical pleasure-loving
life of a nineteenth-century, handsome, upper-class
young man of considerable wealth. Then, after
securing a degree in law and the sciences, he was
commissioned as an officer and went off to fight in the
Crimean War. As he travelled to the front the war
drew to an end, but he arrived at the mud-enveloped
battlefields in time to taste the dereliction, suffering
and squalor of its disease-infested trenches.

Here, where Florence Nightingale toiled to nurse
the sick, Granville Waldegrave experienced the beginning of a dramatic encounter with the living God. It
began when the young nobleman, seized with fear,
suddenly felt overcome by nausea, fever, and weak-
ness. He knew what it meant. He had fallen into the
clutches of the Crimea and was consigned to certain
death by the doctors. 'My last hour has come,' he
thought, 'and I am not ready.'

He had brushed aside the earnest pleas of his
mother to seek God. He had made Harrow and
Oxford hunting grounds for success and personal

pleasure. Now he would have to give an account to God for it all. The physique, mind, and powers which had been lent to him for the duration of life must now be surrendered to God. How would he stand before Him? As he lay on his deathbed, Waldegrave turned his heart and soul over to Christ and asked for His forgiveness. When, to everyone's surprise, he began to recover, he did not forget that prayer. He was already a very different young man.

In a new state of mind the Hon Granville Waldegrave returned to London in time for the beginning of another society season. At first he could not see any great wrong in allowing his time to be consumed by the endless balls, dinners and entertainments of his Belgravia circle. But one evening a prominent barrister who was also a Christian believer took him on one side and asked bluntly, 'What do you do to serve your new Lord and Master?'

Half unwillingly, yet under a strong inner compulsion, Waldegrave began visiting patients at the Middlesex Hospital to read passages from the Bible to them. One of the first men he visited was a Spanish half-caste suffering from a terrible facial cancer, and embittered to the point of hating everyone. As Waldegrave sat by him daily to read and explain portions of the Gospels he saw this man's whole manner become mellowed and transformed by the message of forgiveness and reconciliation with God.

Waldegrave became Lord Radstock when he was only twenty-three, and within two years he was married and installed in Mayfield Park, Southampton, a large mansion nestling in a leafy estate. 'They were both a good deal in society,' wrote Lady Buxton, 'where he was always trying to do his Master's work in a quiet and unobtrusive way. I used to go frequently to their London home in Bryanston Square where Lord and Lady Radstock used to hold Bible study meetings.'

One great step remained to be taken by Lord Radstock before he discovered the purpose for his life. At twenty-six he had taken responsibility for a battalion of infantry volunteers. He recruited, trained and commanded them, and 'Lord Radstock's battalion' became one of the well-known London regiments. Regularly they paraded in Hyde Park — headed by Radstock riding his grey charger. The gaze of Londoners could not fail to be drawn by the elaborate, colourful uniforms provided at Lord Radstock's personal expense.

Then it began to dawn on him that as a Christian his money and resources should be fully at the disposal of his Lord. He was very moved by the faith of Hudson Taylor, the great missionary to China, who was accomplishing so much with so little help from the comfortable Christians at home. Then he looked at himself. An English peer, aged thirty-three, living in luxury and spending most of his money on personal aggrandisement and status symbols. Privately, alone with his Lord in prayer, Radstock gave up his military 'idol' and pledged himself wholly to serve Christ. Free from his commitment to the army, he leapt into every kind of Christian work. He gave large sums to Hudson Taylor's work, became deeply involved with several orphan and immigrant homes, and began to preach at special mission meetings held throughout the country.

London society turned its back on him, for he openly declared its religion a hypocritical sham, its politeness a veneer for jealousy and backbiting, and its addiction to entertainment and pleasure a way of

Lord Radstock

escape from conscience. Lady Buxton again com-
mented, 'He certainly practised what he preached ... I
used to observe how, no doubt to give more money
away, they parted at that time with jewels, china and
carriages one after another.'

Now, unknowingly, Radstock was about to sow
the first seeds of a renewed Christian tradition in the
land of Russia. It happened when he went to speak at
a series of mission meetings held in Weston-super-
Mare in the south west of England. Night after night
the largest public hall in the town was packed out by
thousands of interested people. He spoke about
Christ the Saviour, urging his listeners to repent of
their past sins and come to know Him. One night a
distinguished German physician, Dr Baedeker,
underwent a dramatic conversion to God after listening to Lord Radstock's address. 'I went in,' he
recalled, 'a proud German infidel, and came out a
humble, believing disciple of the Lord Jesus Christ.'

It was Dr Baedeker who, eight years later, went out
as a missionary to Russia. Despite the fact he had only
one lung, a painful curvature of the spine and a weak
heart, he toiled for thirty-two years going from town
to town, visiting every prison in the land and every
convict settlement in the vast wastes of Siberia.
Literally thousands of Christians for many generations must owe their knowledge of the Gospel to the
amazing Dr Baedeker, recognition of whose work
found its way into the books of several Russian
authors, including Tolstoy.

Lord Radstock's own 'missionary' journeys began
when he was thirty-four. A speaking tour took him to
Holland where he drew great crowds wherever he
preached and also made a great impact on the nobility.
Then he went to Paris, centre and jewel of the thriving

French Empire, to encounter the same enthusiastic reception. Wherever he went, however, he felt an irrepressible desire to go to Russia, and before long the way opened up when he received an invitation from a Russian princess. Lord Radstock entered the grand city of St Petersburg — the gathering place of all Russia's nobility and royalty — in 1873. Princess Catherine Galitsin (granddaughter of the man who stirred Tsar Alexander I to seek Christ) recorded her memories of Radstock's arrival:–

'By Heaven's power all doors were thrown open to him — halls, chapels and private houses; whole crowds pressed in to hear the glad tidings. It was just after a week of religious rites that I went to see my cousin, Princess Leiven. There I met Lord Radstock, who had just arrived in St Petersburg.'

At that time, Princess Catherine derived great pleasure from the pomp and splendour of the Russian Orthodox Church ritual, and she told the English peer about the emotion it stirred within her. But Radstock was not prepared to leave her trusting in shallow, emotional feelings drawn from empty ceremonies. He wanted her to know Christ, and told her how she should seek Him. Princess Catherine was thrown into a quandary. Had she been worshipping a mere shadow all her life? Could God really be known? She began to attend every meeting which Lord Radstock held. 'At length,' she wrote, 'after a most blessed sermon, I remained for a private conversation and knelt in prayer before the One Who became my Saviour forever.'

Princess Natalie Leiven of St Petersburg soon followed her cousin in going to Christ for forgiveness of sins and the experience of new life. Day after day Radstock found himself visiting the extravagant draw-

Leningrad — city of palaces: the Anichkov palace

ing rooms of St Petersburg, pressing the aristocracy to
see their need of Christ. Night after night he would be
found preaching through an interpreter to crowded
halls. His conversations with the nobility were always
in French, which was then spoken by all well-placed
members of Russian society.

Almost at once a fashionable St Petersburg newspaper was protesting at the alarming spread of this
evangelical Protestantism. Under the headline: 'A
new apostle in high society,' it described the great
following Lord Radstock had attracted, complaining
bitterly that royal ladies sent him dozens of invitations to hold meetings in their homes. Radstock
himself was filled with amazement by the effects of
his work. 'When I started,' he said, 'several of my
Russian friends thought I had better not go. But I was
able to have six or seven public meetings a week in

French or English, though the greatest part of my time (in all, eight to fourteen hours a day) was occupied in visits to private houses.'

Prince Mechtchersky, the famous Russian satirical writer, wrote a mocking novel entitled 'Lord Apostol' which ridiculed the whole movement. But large numbers of people were finding a transforming power and a peace in Radstock's message which made Mechtchersky's novel seem sour and irrelevant.

One night there sat in Radstock's audience, a man of obvious authority, made all the more awesome by his unusually heavy, black moustache. He was Colonel Paschkoff, the wealthiest army officer in Russia, and one of the most popular members of St Petersburg society. He owned a magnificent palace in the centre of the city, which was crowded with some of the most valuable art treasures in the country. (After the Revolution his home became the French Embassy.)

Listening intently to Lord Radstock, Colonel Paschkoff became aware of the desperate bankruptcy *of his soul*, and began to feel the guilt of all his sinful living. Overcome by a great sense of need, the significance of Christ's death on Calvary came home to him in a new way, and he grasped the truth that he could be given a new life; a new beginning. Like a child he knelt before the Lord in sincere repentance and rose up to the certainty that God had touched and changed his life.

The news of his conversion rocked the nation. From his great wealth, derived from vast estates and from his copper mines in the Ural mountains, the colonel sponsored the distribution of Bibles across the land. Then he threw open his palace to Christian work, and the vast, crimson-velvet ballroom became a

Aristocratic ballrooms became venues for Radstock's preaching

THE 'LORD APOSTOL'   61

gathering point for large numbers of Russians who came together for various Bible study and mission meetings.

Meanwhile the work of Lord Radstock penetrated even into the Russian cabinet. Not far from Colonel Paschkoff lived Count Bobrinsky, a former army Chief-of-Staff and a man of giant intellect. His post in the government was that of Minister of the Interior. He was also an authority on German philosophy and possessed a massive library of philosophical works. Courtesy demanded that the Count attend a dinner which his wife gave in honour of Lord Radstock. When the party had finished dining and retired into the magnificent drawing room, Lord Radstock began speaking to them about Paul's epistle to the Romans. Count Bobrinsky maintained a faintly-amused, largely uninterested expression throughout the talk, but inwardly he was deeply stirred by what he heard.

Afterwards in the privacy of his panelled study, the Count seized a pen and listed all his objections to Radstock's words. So pleased was he with the result that he sent it away for printing. But when he came to read the proofs, he felt that all his protests were hollow and prejudiced. Try as he might he simply could not shake off the feeling that the Englishman was right. Radstock had said that mankind was lost in sin, and that there was no possibility of improvement personally or politically except as individual men and women found Christ. No man could do anything to change himself. Christ alone could cleanse and remake the sinner.

Count Bobrinsky's mental conflict came to an end in earnest prayer to Christ to help, forgive and convert him. 'I found that Jesus was the key, the beginning and the end of all.' Thus, another Russian nobleman committed his all to God's service. Soon after this Count Bobrinsky tried to persuade the novelist Leo Tolstoy to seek conversion, the two men spending eight hours together in continuous, fervent conversation.

Another prominent Russian affected by Lord Radstock's preaching was Count Korff, the Comptroller of the Tsar's court and a confidant of practically every member of the royal family. He listened one evening to a talk in which Radstock explained the sacrificial death of Christ, and came to feel that the punishment due to him for his own sins was borne away on the cross.

'At that time,' recorded Dostoevsky, the writer, 'I happened to hear him preaching in a certain hall; and as I recall I found nothing startling. He spoke neither particularly cleverly nor in a particularly dull manner. And yet he performs miracles over human hearts. People are flocking around him. Many of them are astounded.' Radstock's converts, said Dostoevsky, 'are looking for the poor in order to bestow benefits upon them as quickly as possible. They are ready almost to give away their fortunes.'

When Lord Radstock left St Petersburg after this first, amazing visit, he left a city buzzing with the news of many society people having come to a very personal experience of God. Numerous meetings were started for prayer, Bible study and preaching, and soon efforts to spread Gospel teaching right across the land began in earnest.

The Russian Orthodox Church was decidedly hostile. The Tsar resented the intrusion of 'foreign' religious ideas and was appalled that they had already begun to supplant the ritual of the Orthodox Church in many noble houses. But what could he do? Peasants could be flogged, but what could be done with cabinet ministers and princesses? Princess Leiven, for example, had become hostess-extraordinary to the new movement. Young preachers — Russian and foreign alike — were given free rein in her palace. They used her magnificent Malachite Hall, decorated in green marble, for evangelistic services.

One young preacher supported by the princess founded ten churches, formed numerous Sunday Schools and suggested the building of large evangelical churches in St Petersburg and Moscow, an idea which his wealthy patrons had immediately responded to. The Russian Orthodox hierarchy was further infuriated when these evangelicals secured prominence at the 1877 Moscow Exhibition, Russia's 'window to the world', distributing thousands of items of Gospel literature. But all too soon the hand of persecution was to strike. Princesses *were* arrested and even flogged. Colonel Paschkoff was arrested, stripped of his properties and his great estates in the Urals, and exiled. Many others also were viciously and brutally treated, but not before they had founded churches, printed vast quantities of Bibles and literature, and seen a very great response to their labours at all levels of society in Russia.

Lord Radstock's conversion had made him a man with a very large heart, the evidence of this being the quite extraordinary amount he accomplished in Victorian London in organising help for the disadvantaged. He personally funded the building and operating of several hostels for destitute people — these having a total of nearly 2,000 places. Lord Radstock expended most of his property and income on the kind of charitable enterprises which other members of his social class merely dabbled in.

Noted for his own spartan lifestyle, he sold several properties to buy and convert a very large old hotel to house emigrants from Russia, Scandinavia and Germany. During the early 1880s such immigrant families flooded into London at the rate of hundreds every week. Radstock aimed to save them from immediate squalor and starvation and to look after them until they could find their feet. The immigrants' hostel 'programme' included regular mission meetings which Radstock would conduct personally. In five years 70,000 immigrants passed through his hostel, and many spoke of the spiritual discoveries they had made there.

Lord Radstock also built a conference auditorium near London's Victoria Station, where he himself preached regularly at Sunday services. The Queen Mother drove to some of these meetings, but the regular congregation was fairly small, being mainly composed of the coachmen and servants of that affluent area, which was the community which Radstock had set out to reach with the message of salvation.

Lord Radstock was seen by his friends as a some-what untidy but immensely genial giant whose chief concern was to be communicating to others the spiritual discovery which he made in his youth — the power and reality of Christian conversion. A short time before he died in 1913 he remarked to a friend, 'I have loved the Lord for many years now, but some-how, now that I am an old man, the thought of His unwarranted love to me is almost overpowering.'

Genius at Work
James Clerk Maxwell

THE CLERK MAXWELL family house in Edinburgh was a very strange place. Almost everything in it was designed by 'father', a mildly eccentric barrister with a passion for mechanical things and an amazingly inventive mind. Not long after the birth of James in 1831, his father took it into his head to design a new house to go with all his invented gadgets. So the family moved to their very large and unusual manor in Galloway, and named it 'Glenlair'.

Tragedy struck early at the growing boy, for he was only nine when his mother died of cancer. But his father resolved to do his utmost to make good the loss, and young James grew up to know the closest possible relationship with him. School-days were not an immediate success for the lad who was to become universally regarded as the greatest theoretical physicist of the nineteenth century. He was very shy and seemed rather dull. Most of the time he doodled in his books, drawing elaborate mechanical models which baffled his friends. But then quite suddenly he spurted ahead, capturing all the prizes at his school, the Edinburgh Academy, and astonishing everyone.

Clerk Maxwell was only thirteen when his first

scientific paper was published by the Royal Society of Edinburgh. He had devised a method for constructing perfect oval curves.

As far as religious matters were concerned, James's father had been scrupulous in sending him to church, and he received detailed religious instruction in both the Scottish Presbyterian and Anglican churches. But the budding scientist's religion was of a mechanical and lifeless kind until as a student at Cambridge he grasped and accepted the teaching of the Bible voluntarily and personally. This began when a strong consciousness of inward sinfulness brought him to seek God's forgiveness. He became deeply concerned about pride, self-seeking, envy, deception and secretly-held hostilities, as well as about the outward deeds of sin. It was this view of the inner person — as seen by God — that pressed him to seek genuine forgiveness and a new beginning from God.

'I have the capacity,' he confided to a friend, 'of being more wicked within than any example that man could set me.' But he earnestly believed that Christ's atoning death on the cross of Calvary enabled God to blot out all his sin and worthlessness. So he surrendered his life to Christ, saying that life was nothing without his Saviour. A close student friend at Cambridge recorded that Clerk Maxwell never missed Sunday worship and spent hours in the enjoyment of his Bible.

For Clerk Maxwell life now became filled with joys far surpassing the recreational pleasures of college life. While he was noted for his athletic ability (he was in the habit of double-somersaulting every morning into the river) he was even more noted for his great warmth, and sure character. Those who met with him in his rooms to talk over some problem of life would

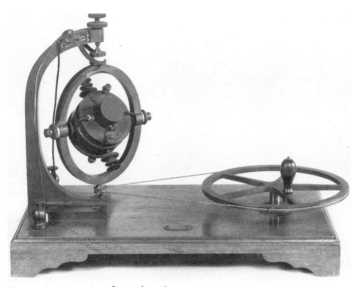

Detecting inertia of an electric current

invariably find themselves guided to the Bible which always lay on the table.

At Cambridge, Clerk Maxwell was at Trinity College where he soon came to be regarded as *the* outstanding scholar. A fellow student (later Master of the College) remembered him in these words: 'When I came up to Trinity, Maxwell was just beginning his second year. His position among us was unique. He was the one acknowledged man of genius among the undergraduates.' Not only did Clerk Maxwell impart an impression of inner strength to people, but original experimental work of the most striking nature poured out of him.

Privately, throughout his student years, he kept up a flow of daily letters to his father who was slowly dying, and he also read volumes of theology, furnishing his mind from the works of such great spiritual writers as John Owen and Jonathan Edwards. These were Clerk Maxwell's favourite authors and his intimate knowledge of their works was well known. As J.C. Crowther wrote, 'His continuously active cultivation of religion, like Faraday's, had a very important relation to the course of his intellectual life.'

At twenty-five Maxwell had to give up the life of a Cambridge don and move to Aberdeen in order to be nearer to his ailing father. The move was made in 1856, when he was appointed Professor of Natural Philosophy at Aberdeen. He was soon to publish brilliant work on Saturn's Rings. The years spent at Aberdeen were highly productive, for Maxwell spent a considerable proportion of his time deeply engrossed in experimental work at Glenlair. Visitors found themselves profoundly impressed not only by his laboratory, but by the morning household prayer meetings at which the eminent young professor would lead his wife, servants and guests in fervent praise. 'Most impressive,' wrote a visiting London physicist, 'and so full of meaning.'

Clerk Maxwell believed that God had endowed human beings with the power to investigate His handiwork, and to harness the power of this created world. This was his motivation for experimental research. God had commanded Adam and Eve saying, *Replenish the earth, and subdue it (Genesis 2.28),* therefore God would surely bless his work and guide his efforts.

At this time Maxwell's highly fertile imagination was extending Faraday's groundwork to thrust forward the understanding of electricity. It was his brilliantly intuitive thinking about electrical currents and the speed of light that led to Hertz's discovery of radio waves. The whole basis of colour photography

Clerk Maxwell

today springs entirely from work that Clerk Maxwell carried out soon after his move to London, where he became Professor of Natural Philosophy and Astronomy at King's College. It was Maxwell who first explained how the addition and subtraction of primary colours produces all other colours. In 1861 he successfully produced the first colour picture using a three-colour process.

The formulae which Clerk Maxwell put forward for calculating various properties of gases remain fundamental to modern physics, and final year university students still grapple with the advanced concepts laid down by this remarkable innovating scientist.

The greatest period of Clerk Maxwell's scientific life began when he was persuaded to move back to Cambridge to be the first Professor of Experimental Physics. At Cambridge he founded the famous Cavendish Laboratory. The Cambridge academic circle had a deep and warm regard for the black-bearded, quiet professor so devoid of any trace of pomposity. He rarely laughed, but the twinkle was seldom out of his eye. For light relief he used to write satirical verses, some of them lampooning the theory of evolution. (More seriously he published an acclaimed mathematical refutation of the 'nebular hypothesis' of LaPlace, and dismissed with great effect the evolutionary arguments of the pro-Darwin writer Herbert Spencer.)

It is very significant that Clerk Maxwell's predictions about the theory of evolution have been perfectly fulfilled. In writing once to an English bishop he expressed sorrow that 'conjectural scientific hypotheses' should be 'fastened to the text in *Genesis*'. As he foresaw, an increasingly discredited theory of organic evolution survives today only because it is needed to bolster modern man's unbelief in God.

The finest source of information about Clerk Maxwell's spiritual life is found in letters written to his 'strictly unmathematical' wife whenever he was away. Sometimes he would relate the events of Sunday. 'I have just come from hearing Mr Baptist Noel. The church was full to standing and the whole service was as plain as large print. The exposition was the Parable of the Talents and the sermon was on *John 3.16...*'

Frequently he muses on walking closely with God in a real experience of His presence. 'I can always have you with me in my mind — why should we not have our Lord always in our minds for we have His life, character and mind far more clearly described than we can know anyone here? Pray to Him for a constant sight of Him, for He is man that we might be able to look to Him, and God so that He can create us anew in His own image.'

In a time of trial he wrote to his wife: 'May the Lord preserve you from all the evil that assaults you, to work out His own purposes . . . I have been back at *1 Corinthians 13.* Read it along with *1 John 4* from verse 7 to the end, or, if you like, the whole epistle and *Mark 12.28.* Think what God has decided to do to all those who submit themselves to His righteousness and are willing to receive His gift. They are to be conformed to the image of His Son. As surely as we receive Him now so will we be made conformable to His image. Let us begin by taking no thought about worldly cares and setting our minds on the righteousness of God and His kingdom — and then we shall have far clearer views about the worldly cares them-

Maxwell's apparatus in the Cavendish Laboratory

selves and we shall be enabled to fight them under Him Who has overcome the world.'

This first ever Professor of Experimental Physics died from cancer at the young age of forty-eight, leaving behind him an unsurpassed contribution to physics and mathematics. In 1873 Clerk Maxwell had published his *Treatise on Electricity and Magnetism*, which presented a comprehensive theoretical and mathematical framework for the understanding of the electromagnetic field, energy and light. Albert Einstein described this accomplishment as 'the most profound and most fruitful that physics has experienced since the time of Newton.'

Maxwell also created the vital mathematical basis for the 'kinetic theory of gases' following years of experimentation by himself and his wife. Not surprisingly Professor C. Domb said, 'Most modern physicists would probably agree in naming James Clerk Maxwell as the scientist of the nineteenth century who made the greatest contribution to the remarkable advances in physics of our time.'

The Biographical Dictionary of Scientists (London, 1984) provides the following succinct summary of Clerk Maxwell's achievements:

'Maxwell is generally considered to be the greatest theoretical physicist of the 1800s, as his forebear Faraday was the greatest experimental physicist. His rigorous mathematical ability was combined with great insight to enable him to achieve brilliant syntheses of knowledge in the two most important areas of physics at that time. In building on Faraday's work to discover the electromagnetic nature of light, Maxwell not only explained electromagnetism but paved the way for the discovery and application of the whole spectrum of electromagnetic radiation that has

characterised modern physics. In developing the kinetic theory of gases, Maxwell gave the final proof that
the nature of heat resides in the motion of molecules.'

Such was the quality of the great scientist's life and
the reality of his walk with God, that *Nature* com-
mented in an obituary: 'His simple Christian faith
gave him a peace too deep to be ruffled by bodily pain
or external circumstances.' This was the testimony left
when the 'quiet genius' travelled on — to the day he
had looked forward to above all others.

The Heart of a Hymnwriter
Philip P. Bliss

A CENTURY AND A HALF ago the forest covered mountains of Northern Pennsylvania were a rugged but welcome refuge for penniless couples seeking a home and a living. There, in a wild and remote region, John Bliss and his wife built themselves a simple log cabin and set about the backbreaking task of earning their livelihood from the forest. It was in this simple shack, miles from anywhere, that their first child was born in the summer of 1838. Philip Paul Bliss — destined to be one of America's great soul-winners and hymnwriters — began life amidst the biting poverty and loneliness of the backwoods.

However, there was an atmosphere and a strength in that household which more than compensated for all its material hardships. When Philip Bliss looked back on his youth he described it in these words: 'Whatever of plain living, small home, or poor advantages I had in my childhood, I cherish this precious thought — my parents prayed for me even before I knew the meaning of prayer, and consecrated me to the Lord and His service. My father lived in continual communion with his Saviour. He was a poor man, but early in the morning as well as after the toil of the day,

sitting in the porch of his humble home, his voice would be heard in song.

'My mother used sometimes to say laughingly that all his hymns commenced with the word "Come". I can remember many of them — "Come, ye sinners, poor and needy", "Come ye that love the Lord", and "Come in my partners in distress". He was a diligent reader of the Bible and had the most implicit faith in its teachings. My first recollection of him is his daily family prayer. Devout and tender, he repeated year after year about the same words until we all knew them by heart. His prayers were very real to me in my childhood.'

The hardship and seclusion of Bliss's mountain home helped forge within him the strength and quietness of character which were to become his most arresting and compelling qualities as a man. Barefoot and wearing heavily patched clothes, he grew up to help his mother grow vegetables for sale in the nearest village, and later to labour with his father in the cutting and hauling of timber. In his spare time he would wander alone in the silent forest — utterly absorbed by the sounds of nature. Bliss's exceptional musical faculty found early expression. He was only seven when he made an entirely original wind instrument from reeds, so that he could play the tunes of birds and forest animals.

In later life he often related his first encounter with any other musical instrument. He was just ten years old, and had walked several miles through the forest to the nearest village. 'A barefooted mountain lad had gone, as was his custom, to the little village with his basket of vegetables which he peddled from door to door. One day, having sold his stock, he was on his way home when the sound of music was wafted to his ear through the open door of a house by the way. He paused: the music continued and drew him nearer and nearer, until quite unconsciously the fascinated boy had entered the veranda doors into a room. There, a lady was playing the piano. Entranced, he stood listening, his very soul lost in delight. He had never heard such music before. Suddenly some slight movement of his attracted the lady's attention. She turned, and with a scream of surprise shouted, "What are you doing in my house? Get out of here — with your great bare feet!"'

'Ah,' Bliss would say as he related this event, 'my feet are large — but God gave them to me.'

Like most of the boys in the forests Bliss worked morning and evening, and went to the village school several afternoons a week. His first job outside his own household was on a farm at the age of thirteen. As far as his faith was concerned, he could not recall a time when he was not 'sorry for sin, and did not love Christ'. Very early, out of the reach of memory's conscious arm, Bliss had been brought to know the Lord in a real and personal way. But there came a time when he dedicated his life to his Saviour in a deeper way than ever before — and that was following a religious awakening among his school fellows. He was fourteen at the time, and working away from home in order to attend a better school in a bigger village.

Educationally Bliss made exceptional progress for a forest boy, and at the age of nineteen took his first long journey to Towanda Town, all his worldly goods tied up in a linen bag. At Towanda he hoped to earn his passage through a college course. His first letter home reads: 'There is a chance of my getting all the jobs of work I want to do which will pay my way.

Philip Bliss

Board, lodging, washing, light and fuel, room rent included, cost me two dollars a week... I am a kind of chore-boy, but I am not ashamed of it. I saw wood, bring water, and sweep rooms at so much a piece. The college steward says: "Come along to school and if you cannot pay me now, pay me after you have earned it." I have taken up Grammar, Algebra, Physiology and Latin.'

In a short time he also took up music, graduating from the one-year course to become a part-time schoolmaster at a little village academy at Rome, Pennsylvania. Besides teaching, he worked as a farm labourer. Anxious to help his family, Bliss paid for his younger sister to live with a family in the village and attend classes at the academy. He was to reap more from his thoughtfulness than he ever could have anticipated, for his sister was soon befriended by a senior pupil, eighteen-year-old Lucy Young. One friendship led to another, and after about a year, Philip Bliss could write in his diary, 'June 1st 1859: married Miss Lucy T. Young, the very best thing I could have done.'

He had only been married a matter of months when his attention was caught by a newspaper article describing a six-week intensive course in music to be held in New York. The course would consist of lectures and lessons given by the country's leading musicians — and would lead on to further such courses. Bliss longed to be able to attend such an event, but the cost was utterly beyond him. He practically walked on air when his wife's grandmother produced a secret 'silver-dollar savings stocking' containing enough money in it to cover the fees. She insisted that he enrol.

On his return home from tuition in New York, Bliss decided to set up as a travelling music teacher. Armed with an accordion, among various other instruments, and aided by a large but slightly lame horse (the best he could afford) he went to different villages providing 'music schools' at very moderate cost. For over three years he maintained a highly successful 'circuit', while living in the village of Rome. Wherever he went he became noted not only for his amazing ability to teach children to sing, but for his earnest words of testimony. At home he was superintendent of a vigorous Sunday School — his fervent speaking many times causing visiting pastors to urge him to enter the ministry.

At this stage of his life the young man's own

remarkable singing voice had been noticed by at least one notable critic, who heard him singing scales: 'Beginning with E flat, or even D flat below, he would, without apparent effort, produce a series of clarion tones, in an ascending series, until having reached the D (fourth tenor clef) I would look to see him weaken. But no, he would go on, taking D sharp, E, F, F sharp and G, without a sound of straining nor the usual apoplectic look of effort.'

Bliss saved hard during those years as a travelling teacher, for he had a burning ambition to bring his parents out of the backwoods hut which had been their lifelong home, to a cottage in Rome. Eventually a cottage was bought and father Bliss came to view the new home. His son took the grey-haired old man by pony and trap along to the street which would be his place of retirement. He asked him to guess which house would be his. The old man pointed to a very modest house — but he was wrong. Then he indicated another, and another, each time selecting a humbler building. Bliss could contain himself no longer. Turning the trap round he drove back to a *new* cottage fronted with blossoming lilacs, and lifted his father down to view his new home.

After five years of married life, earning his living as a travelling teacher, Bliss and his family moved to Chicago. From this base Philip Bliss's work as a teacher and tutor took him to homes and academies all over the North West of America. By now he was a prolific composer and had also produced a number of hymns for children. His heart was very much in children's work, as his new church in Chicago quickly realised. Before long he was superintendent of a Sunday School which grew to enormous proportions. Bliss had an impressive ability to communicate with children and young people, coupled with tremendous affection for them and their spiritual needs.

His passion for reaching the unconverted brought him to the notice of D. L. Moody, whom he frequently helped in his evangelistic meetings. But it was an association formed with another travelling preacher, Major W. D. Whittle, which took Bliss into whole-time Christian service.

Major Whittle, a former member of General Howard's staff in the American Civil War, had suffered the loss of his right arm, and had been taken prisoner of war. While recovering from his wound in hospital he began to read the New Testament, and his eyes were opened to the meaning of the Gospel. It was as he read *Romans* chapter 6 that he understood intellectually the doctrine of justification by faith alone. One night Major Whittle was awakened by a male nurse who asked him to pray for a boy dying in the ward. The nurse confessed he was an ungodly man and could not pray himself. 'I can't pray either,' said the major, 'I have never prayed in my life. I am just as you are.'

'Can't pray!' exclaimed the nurse, 'I thought from seeing you read the New Testament that you were a praying man. I can't go back to him alone — come and see him.'

Whittle went down the ward to find an eighteen-year-old soldier pleading for prayer. He knew he was dying and told of his background in a Bible-teaching Sunday School. But he had turned away from it all and was now terrified of death.

'I dropped on my knees,' recorded Whittle, 'took his hand and in a few broken words I confessed my own sins and asked God for Christ's sake to forgive me. I believe right there that He did forgive me and I became His child. Then I prayed earnestly for the boy. He became quiet and pressed my hand as I pleaded God's promises. When I rose from my knees he was dead. A look of peace was upon his face and I can but believe that God used me to get his attention fixed on Christ and to lead him to trust in His precious blood.'

Major Whittle (who wrote the hymn 'I know not why God's wondrous grace to me hath been made known') invited Bliss to his Chicago home for fellowship, and a close friendship immediately sprang into being. The contribution which Bliss was to make to the preaching tours of Major Whittle was of a vastly different character from the activities of so many American 'song leaders'. Dr Gardiner, the pastor of his Chicago church expressed it in these words:

'Too often the Lord's house is turned into a concert hall and the service of song made a device for filling pews. The minister comes to his duties in the pulpit after the world and the flesh and the devil have set things moving to their liking. Little wonder that preaching in such circumstances saves few souls. It is like expecting harvest with the enemy invited to go before the reaper sowing tares, and to follow him snatching away the seed. To those who knew anything of Bliss, it will be unnecessary to say that he had no sympathy with such ideas. He shared the feeling that the disposition to make the song and service of God's house showy and entertaining was an abomination in God's sight.'

So he believed that all who led in the service of song should sing with grace in their hearts and that the music should be strictly spiritual. Many times he would say, 'When we sing, let us forget everything but the Cross. Let us seek to have the people lose sight of us, of our efforts, and think only of Him Who died.' The kind of meeting he arranged for the presentation of the message of the Gospel steered well away from the remotest similarity with secular entertainment. For Philip Bliss, services of worship, and meetings for the preaching of the Gospel, had to be serious and weighty, characterised by reverence, awe and the challenging of needy souls.

Bliss believed with his whole heart in the possibility of the early conversion of children. He aimed to have all understand that Christ was the children's Saviour, and that in their tenderest years little ones might know God's life-changing power and become truly converted Christians.

Next to the Word of God, he felt the instrumentality of song important for children — and he used it. Many times he would stop in the middle of a song to explain what happened on the Cross, emphasising the love of Jesus, and pleading with every heart. As he did so there would be tears in his voice, and wonderful pathos and sweetness. No school ever had a superintendent who held a larger place in the children's hearts than he, and it was easy to see why — he was a lover of children. Wherever he was he could not help gathering about him the little four and five year-olds and talking to them in a way that every one of them understood. Whatever he said was 'law' and 'Gospel' in the fullest sense.

Bliss, while still following his occupation as a music teacher, frequently joined Major Whittle to sing and speak at his evangelistic meetings. But he was constantly subjected to persuasive appeals to give up his work and commit himself entirely to the evangelist's missionary efforts. His own progress as a mission speaker had been considerable. As a consultant teacher he was now earning substantial fees. As a conductor of various choral societies and orchestras he was in great demand. The Handel and Haydn Society of San Francisco had offered $3,000 a year for his services (a top salary in those days) and other leading national orchestras showed close interest in the Chicago musician. As a powerful bass-baritone, a composer, or more especially as an orchestrator and conductor, Bliss was assured of success.

However, he came to the definite conviction that he must serve God full-time. Once he and his wife had taken their decision, they would never permit a word to be spoken concerning the opportunities declined, because they counted them all as refuse compared with the satisfaction of being servants of Christ. The Whittle-Bliss evangelistic meetings attracted in their day large numbers of listeners. They preached (and Bliss sang) to crowded halls, keeping closely to the plain proclamation of the soul-saving truths of the Gospel.

Bliss himself would invariably take additional meetings aimed specifically at children. His huge frame and long beard might have been a fearsome sight to some children, but his unique warmth and gentleness of manner gave him very real help in expressing to them the meaning of grace. He wrote many hymns, often misused as adult hymns when in fact he intended them solely for little children. Nevertheless, even some of his simplest pieces contain solid thought.

Wherever the Whittle-Bliss meetings went the testimonies of local pastors were the same. They were noted for their marked simplicity and great earnestness. They worked in an atmosphere of real tenderness for souls, and if they often over-stressed

their appeals to the heart, they did so because of their utter genuineness and concern that people might be saved. Again and again pastors put on record the moving character of their meetings. Bliss himself seems to have made little use of public invitations although Major Whittle invariably gave one when he was preaching.

At Chautauqua, Bliss took to the open air, thousands standing out in moonlit evening meetings to hear him sing his hymns of testimony, and then preach. On one occasion when Bliss was conducting services at a church in Jackson he was invited by the Michigan State Prison to speak to the eight hundred prisoners. When he preached and sang to them in the morning he was so moved by the drawn, dissolute and embittered expressions of so many of the men that he resolved to have something for them by the evening meeting.

Eyewitnesses put on record that the most melting scene they had ever witnessed was that of Bliss appealing to the men in the terms of the Gospel, and then singing his own newly-written hymn, so slowly and earnestly:

> *Man of sorrows! What a name*
> *For the Son of God, Who came*
> *Rebel sinners to reclaim!*
> *Hallelujah, what a Saviour!*

A large body of the prisoners were quite shaken and broken down, and the 'persuasive appeal of love' in the Gospel must surely have yielded its own fruit.

Philip Bliss unquestionably stood for the infallibility of the Bible as God's revealed Word. He believed firmly in the total depravity — the deep sinfulness — of men and women in the sight of Almighty God, and

their utter inability to please Him, unless freely
forgiven by Jesus Christ Who suffered in the place of
guilty sinners. He believed that the hearts of men and
women are so hard and rebellious, that the softening
and convicting work of the Holy Spirit is vital to
bring them to repent and seek the Lord. He insisted
on the necessity of personal conversion, this being a
radical transformation of life brought about by the
power of God, and leading to an intimate walk with
Him. Philip Bliss also emphasised the biblical teaching that the genuinely converted person is eternally
saved, as salvation can never be lost.

To the modern outlook, Bliss might sometimes
appear over-sentimental, especially if his children's
hymns are judged as if they were meant for adults.
But he possessed a largeness of heart and a desire for
souls which is seldom seen even among fervent
Christians.

Bliss and his wife came to the end of life's uncertain
journey unexpectedly early. He was 38, and his wife
36, when their heavenly Father took them to their
eternal home. They had just spent the Christmas of
1876 at their home town of Rome, Pennsylvania.
Then, leaving their two small children with an aunt,
they boarded the Pacific Express bound for Chicago,
in order to take part in special New Year services. A
blizzard raged as two great locomotives hauled the
express across the giant Ashtabula Viaduct in Ohio,
seventy feet above a frozen river.

Suddenly, with the passenger coaches still crossing
the viaduct, the whole structure gave way, hurling
the coaches into the ravine amidst a crescendo of
grinding, crashing girders and beams. One survivor
believed that Philip Bliss was seen among the tangled
coaches, trying to locate and free his trapped wife. It

was supposed that in failing to save her, he stayed to comfort her, and they perished together in the fire that swept through the wreckage. Whether or not this was so it was impossible to verify, for the couple were among the hundred or so people whose bodies were either never recovered or could not be identified.

'They have gone,' said Major Whittle, 'as absolutely and completely gone as if translated like Enoch.'

The last words that had passed the lips of Philip Bliss as he pleaded with sinners were the words of his own hymn:

I know not the hour when my Lord shall come
To take me away to His own dear home,
But I know that His presence will lighten the gloom,
*   And that will be glory for me.*

Everywhere in the United States believers were moved to mourning by the death of this godly couple. 'Dear Bliss,' said a leading New York pastor, 'the memories will come — his face, his noble form, his gentle manners, his fervent prayers and appeals, his deep absorption in the one work of his life. The world seems lonely without him.'

What an example he had been of the power of God in the life of a dedicated believer. He had certainly striven for the standards of his own hymn of consecration to God which he called, 'My Prayer' —

More holiness give me,
*   More strivings within;*
More patience in suffering,
*   More sorrow for sin;*
More faith in my Saviour,
*   More sense of His care;*
More joy in His service,
*   More purpose in prayer.*

More gratitude give me,
More trust in the Lord;
More pride in His glory,
More hope in His Word;
More tears for His sorrows,
More pain at His grief;
More meekness in trial,
More praise for relief.

More purity give me,
More strength to o'ercome;
More freedom from earth stains,
More longings for home;
More fit for the kingdom,
More used would I be;
More blessed and holy,
More, Saviour, like Thee.

Brewer who Renounced a Fortune
Fred Charrington

THE VAST BREWERY OF Charrington and Head dominated Victorian London's East End. Its colossal ladders, towers and storehouses stood gauntly above the squalid, overcrowded houses of the Mile End Road. From its cobbled courtyards poured a constant stream of barrel-laden carts, taking the flow of 'Entire' ale to the hundreds of pubs in the great Charrington empire.

Most breweries of that time were owned and run by millionaire families who claimed a very high degree of respectability and held important positions in public life. The Charringtons were no exception. The head of the family, a tall, erect figure, who would have passed as a colonel in a guards regiment, was particularly well-known as a prominent layman in the Church of England. He was very proud of the size, wealth, and efficiency of his business, and seemed totally indifferent to the tidal wave of human misery which it had unleashed on the Victorian poorer classes. Frederick, his eldest son, was groomed to follow him as head of the firm.

Marlborough and Brighton College had both taken a hand in shaping the younger Charrington for his future, while extensive continental travel had been chosen to expand his mind. To round off his education he had spent a year apprenticed to the management of the Queen's brewer at Windsor. Then he was ready to enter the enormous family business which he would one day inherit. Tall and powerfully built like his father, Fred Charrington revelled in open-air sports, horsemanship, plenty of action, and foreign travel.

In quieter vein he was a regular churchgoer, though of course, he would not have been found listening to 'emotional' and 'over-personal' preaching, which his family disdained. It was the elegant, scholarly, tasteful preaching of upper-class parish churches which soothed the souls of wealthy brewers. How strange it was, young Charrington once thought, that even some of the upper classes could go in for the 'baser' sort of religion. One of his closest friends, the future Lord Garvagh, had recently surprised him with the statement that he had become 'saved'!

Fred Charrington's plan was to let the clergymen arrange his passport to Heaven for that was their function. His role was to conquer and enjoy life, and in this spirit he soon grasped the reins of management at his father's brewery. During the damp, dark months of winter, the quest for pleasure took him to the South of France. It was here, while walking in Cannes, that Charrington fell into conversation with another wealthy young Englishman who had gone south in quest of the sun — William Rainsford. A firm friendship soon developed as the pair continued their Riviera holiday together.

When they returned home to London Charrington invited his new friend to stay at his father's Wimbledon mansion. As they relaxed for the evening in deep leather chairs, sharing reminiscences, Rainsford suddenly said, 'I feel very guilty, Fred. We have travelled together all the way over the continent and enjoyed ourselves very much, but I have never spoken to you about your soul. The fact is, I am a Christian, but I have spent the winter in the South of France for my health and I have been in very worldly society.'

Charrington was astonished. 'Really Rainsford,' he protested, 'we have had a very good time on the continent and I think it is a great pity and in very poor taste that you bring up such a debatable subject just now.'

Rainsford looked disappointed and guilty. Clearly he could not pursue the matter. 'I only ask one thing of you,' he said hesitatingly to Charrington. 'When I have left, promise me you will read through the third chapter of John's Gospel.'

Charrington promised, and that night, with mingled curiosity and impatience, he kept his promise. Just before going to bed he put on his dressing gown, lit a pipe, and sat down with his Bible. 'This is a very curious thing indeed,' he thought. 'Here are two men, my new friend Rainsford and my old friend Lord Garvagh, and both say the same thing — that they are saved.' As he read the promised chapter, particularly the words, *He that believeth on the Son hath everlasting life,* Charrington suddenly realised that true Christianity was not a facade of respectability, bolstered up by church attendance, but a living contact with the Lord God. His friends had come to believe and to know the Son. In a moment the young brewer found himself despising his sinfulness and selfishness. Alone in his bedroom he bowed his head, believed in Christ as Saviour and felt an immediate and overwhelming sense that Christ had received him.

'Thank God,' he said later, 'when I was twenty years old I became a Christian. I was born again.'

Charrington's outlook on life became vastly changed, and with an anxiety to do something worthwhile and useful, he started helping a friend who ran an evening school for illiterate working boys. At the same time a very troubling thought kept rubbing against his now tender conscience. The brewery business had so many wretched, objectionable implications. Was it really right? One night, on his way to the evening class, Charrington was passing *The Rising Sun*, a filthy pub in a narrow, East End street, when he caught sight of a poorly-clad woman with two little children clutching on to her skirt and crying with hunger. She went up to the pub door and called to her husband inside. Her plea for money seared into Charrington's mind.

A man appeared, and for a moment he stood staring at her. Suddenly he rushed out and savagely knocked his wife and children down in the street. 'What did I do about it?' recalled Charrington in later years. 'Well, I was just a coward, for sin makes cowards of us all. I looked up at the sign over the door and there, emblazoned in gilt letters was my own name. How could I do anything when I was responsible for it all? It suddenly flashed into my mind that this was only one case of misery and brutality in one of the hundreds of pubs our firm possessed. What an appalling amount of wretchedness and degradation our enormous business must cause. It was a crushing realisation.

'There and then, without any hesitation, I said in my mind to the drunken husband, "You have knocked your own wife down and with the same blow you have knocked me out of the brewery

Ion Falconer and Fred Charrington (standing)

business."' It was a decision which cost its maker an
income of £1,000 per week — a vast fortune in those
days — as well as the major stake in London's largest
brewery. When old Mr Charrington heard of his son's
intention, he was both amazed and deeply insulted.
What folly was this? It verged on madness.

As they talked long and furiously together, the
father protested that his son was pitting the emotion

of a few minutes spent in the East End slums against his own lifelong study of the drink question. Should operating theatres or medical schools be abolished because medical students suffered fainting and nausea when they saw their first operation? His son, he contended, had merely suffered a kind of temporary nausea. Mr Charrington set out to brew the best beer in the country, but did not believe he should be held responsible for the action of fools. He didn't ask a man to drink more of his beer than he could. Furthermore he felt that condemning breweries on account of drunkards was no different from condemning religion because there were religious maniacs. However, Fred Charrington could not be persuaded to stay, so his father, deeply shocked and offended, accepted his resignation and cut him out of the family will. The prospect of a vast inheritance was gone for ever.

Shortly after, old Mr Charrington was thrown from his horse while out riding, sustaining injuries from which he never recovered. When he was on his deathbed, with the members of the family gathered round him, the dying man said, 'You all go out of the room for a little time — let Fred remain with me alone. He is the only one who knows about these things.'

'You are right, Fred,' he said when they were alone. 'You have chosen the better part, which will never be taken away.' Then father and son prayed together.

By the time his father died Fred Charrington had already become involved in an evangelistic meeting which started in a hayloft over a stable just off the Mile End Road in London's East End. Every evening of the week a crowd of boys climbed the rickety stairs to take their places on rough benches. There, by the yellow light of paraffin lamps, the Bible was opened and the Gospel preached. Even then Charrington knew for certain that this was his life's work — reaching the lost. When he led the fledgling boys' mission into a properly converted schoolroom a year or two later, over three hundred filled the premises night after night. Even the notorious Whitechapel Gang (membership of which was restricted to youths convicted of stealing) were caught in his net. They planned, one night, to smash the hall and beat up the occupants, but they ended up listening to the stentorian preaching of Charrington — many of them visibly cut to the heart by the message of Christ.

One night, after Charrington had closed his meeting and most of the boys had gone, he noticed a nine-year-old sitting in a corner helplessly crying. A few questions brought his unhappy story tumbling out. He was one of a large family living with their widowed mother in a single top floor attic. There was no work for any of them, no money, and now everything they had of value had been sold. He had come to the meeting because he could get some tea and some warmth. When Charrington took the boy home he found such hardship that he decided immediately to expand his work to help all workless boys. He bought an old bottling warehouse, converted it into a boys' home, and called it the 'Tower Hamlets Shoeblack and Woodchopping Brigade'. Any boy accommodated by him went out with the organised working parties, many of them earning not only their keep, but a life-saving contribution for their impoverished families.

The mission work could not possibly restrict itself to boys for long. It did not have to. A wealthy Christian landlord, deeply impressed with the work

going on, donated the cost of a six-hundred seat mission hall, which came into use in 1872. Now there was no holding Fred Charrington in his exhaustive efforts to get his message into the homes of the people. He was joined by a Cambridge languages student (later to become a leading university academic) the Hon Ion Keith-Falconer, son of the Earl of Kintore.

At the time Ion Falconer, a tall, slim, fair-haired young man, was a leading amateur racing cyclist, having defeated the British professional champion by five yards. He was due to compete in a university championship on the very day that he responded to God's call to give himself to the Tower Hamlets work. He felt there should be no looking back, and immediately wired the course umpire: 'I have made up my mind not to run having started the race of *Hebrews 12.1-2.*'

With Charrington he preached both in the mission hall and in the open air until their congregations had so increased that a piece of ground had to be rented and a massive tent erected. The tent, a round white monster, lit at night by great chandeliers, was almost always packed. Audiences of 1,400 listened to Charrington or an invited preacher of note. To reach still greater crowds with the Gospel, Charrington rented both Lusby's and Forester's Music Halls every Sunday evening, so that an aggregate congregation of five thousand listened to invited evangelical preachers in the East End.

It was in connection with music halls that Charrington's name really became a household word at the turn of the century. He was speaking one day to a man who had come to him in great agony of mind. 'Are you a married man?' he had asked. 'No,' came the reply, 'those reptiles at Lusby's have ruined my wife.' Charrington had long been aware of the large-scale prostitution organised on music hall premises. But now he was moved to get something done about it. As with obscene literature nowadays, the law clearly covered the situation which prevailed, but the law was hardly ever enforced.

The Tower Hamlets Mission began a full-scale campaign against this blatant prostitution. Tirelessly they stood outside music halls distributing tracts, speaking personally to known prostitutes, and cautioning young people seen going in and out. They were ridiculed in the press. Charrington was cartooned holding his 'moral microscope', and the music hall proprietors paid thugs to assault and molest his co-workers. Because he did not succeed in getting the police to act, Charrington put himself forward for election as the London County Councillor for Mile End, and won the seat. As a councillor he was able to smash the main vice rings and sweep the worst brothels out of the East End.

Charrington's Sunday congregations had grown so large that the erection of the Great Assembly Hall in the Mile End Road became a dire necessity. Charles Haddon Spurgeon advised them to go ahead with it. R. C. L. Bevan, head of Barclays Bank, offered a very large sum of money, and Lord Shaftesbury and Samuel Morley MP followed suit.

The Great Assembly Hall was built inside ten months and opened in 1886. With yellow-tinted windows, bright orange decorations, two galleries and five thousand seats, it was the second largest place of worship in London. Justifiably it became known as 'The Hall of Stirring Memories'. Once open, meetings were held in the great hall every single night for the next fifty years. Every Saturday night there was the great prayer meeting, when men and women who had been converted through the preaching of the mission would give testimonies and pray together. Every Sunday evening a vast audience would gather for a 'Gospel Service' which always opened with the hymn 'Sinners Jesus will receive'.

The people were attracted into the services by many different means. Open-air preaching, tract distribution, daily door-to-door visitation, a heavy programme of poor relief, and a regular Sunday after-noon procession round the streets were all employed to arouse the attention of London's East Enders.

Then came the start of a new challenge. Professor Falconer wrote: 'During the hard times of last winter a work was forced upon our mission which we had never contemplated. The distress of that winter was extreme and for many weeks we opened our halls and fed the literally starving multitudes with dry bread and cocoa. Our feeding became a very publicised matter and we were enabled to give no less than 20,000 meals from January to February.'

From that moment the work of feeding hungry families became one of the principal activities of the mission. In due course Charrington persuaded the dignitaries of the City of London to inaugurate the annual Lord Mayor's Banquet for the East End poor. Regular weekly meals also became available, support coming from many sources, including the king. Through the terrible recession of the 1920s, hundreds of hungry poor could count on the Great Assembly Hall of the Tower Hamlets Mission for relief.

The extent of Charrington's work and its influence on London's East End was far too extensive to be captured in a brief biography. Supreme among his

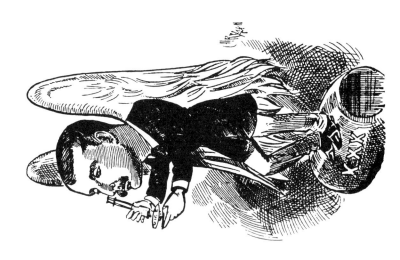

labours was his preaching and evangelising, bringing lost souls to a personal knowledge of Christ, and to an everlasting inheritance on high. Then there was his tireless temperance work, which delivered countless East End homes from the brutality and misery arising from drunkenness. In addition, the homes and work stations for destitute boys and girls saved thousands from degradation and neglect. Beyond that, the regular poor relief work fed and clothed over a thousand families every week during the years of greatest shortage.

Charrington was a tremendous 'character' who always aimed high in seeking to accomplish things for the Lord. His ingenuity and daring were considerable, as when he brought to a halt the sale of alcoholic beverages in Parliament during the First World War. The king had declared an abstention period in the royal palaces for the duration of the war, and Charrington successfully argued that the Houses of Parliament were the royal 'Palaces of Westminster', and should therefore observe the king's resolution.

His method of persuading the Lord Mayor of London to sponsor free meals for the East End poor was no less ingenious. Charrington's initial attempts to raise benevolent funds from the City fell on deaf ears. Then, one year, he arranged a great charity meal to be served right opposite the venue of the Lord Mayor's Banquet, on the very same day. Having secured sponsorship for the charity meal from the king (who knew nothing of the date or place) Charrington emblazoned the front of his hired hall with a streamer proclaiming the king's free bounty for the poor. It was intended to give the maximum embarrassment to the wealthy City fraternity, and it succeeded. It succeeded also in opening the Lord

Mayor's purse — and those of leading business houses — to the sponsoring of regular food aid for poor families.

Fred Charrington died in 1936, while still very much on the 'active list' of the army of the King of kings, having superintended the work he had founded for sixty-eight years. London has seldom seen such a light blazing for the Gospel, nor such a ministry of compassion as that operated by the brewer who found Christ, and gave up a fortune to serve Him.

Spearhead into the Unknown
Lord Kelvin

AMONG THE SELECT BAND of pioneer scientists dramatically pushing back the frontiers of knowledge in the nineteenth century, one particularly caught the public imagination by his astonishing number of innovations and inventions. Lord Kelvin — as he became — branded his name into theoretical research by formulating in precise terms the First and Second Laws of Thermodynamics, and by such concepts as the Absolute Temperature Scale. But his name became a household word with his submarine cable exploits, and with his revolutionary ship's compass — to mention just one of his seventy patented brainwaves.

Born in Ulster as William Thomson, the future physicist was a professor's son. His father was a mathematician who authored a textbook which ran through no less than seventy editions. The family of four sons and three daughters lived in a roomy house on the outskirts of Belfast, their childhood happiness being marred only by the suffering of their sick mother.

William was six when one evening the housekeeper took them all into their father's large first-floor study. 'He was sitting there alone at the side of the fire,'

wrote Elizabeth, the eldest girl. 'As the little troop
came into the room he opened his arms wide and we
ran into them, and he said, "We have no mother
now." And there we stayed in his arms until the
embers burned out.'

'Where will the children's nursery be now that their
mother is gone?' asked the housekeeper.

'In my own bedroom,' came the reply, and the beds
of the two youngest boys were placed beside his own.
Professor Thomson had made up his mind that he
would be father and mother and schoolmaster to his
children. Every morning he would take them on a
pre-breakfast walk, when he would tell them stories
of travel and discovery. Every afternoon, university
lectures being over, he would give them lessons. And
every night he would read to them. 'Our father read
with us regularly every Sunday morning some chap-
ters from the Old Testament and in the evening some
from the New.'

William later recalled that all the English, Maths
Geography and Classics he ever learned as a boy, he
learned at home. 'I never met a better teacher in
anything than my father was in everything,' and
'everything' included the faith of the Bible; the message of the Lord Jesus Christ, Who was Professor
Thomson's Saviour, Friend and Guide. This was
William Thomson's home background; first in Belfast
and later in a quaint stone-built professor's house in
the University of Glasgow to which the family
moved.

It was 1841 when seventeen-year-old William
travelled down to Cambridge by mail coach to begin
five years of study there. Unlike many other famous
Christian believers, there is no trace of any clear-cut
religious 'crisis' in his life, but a consistent stream of

Kelvin's original divided ring electrometer

evidence demonstrates that from boyhood he held
very deep convictions which dominated his manner of
life and his character.

Tall, very dark and heavily built, William Thomson's student days were marked by the unusual physical vigour he brought to everything he did. And at the end of his degree studies he captured sufficient prizes to be able to afford a tour of the laboratories of the foremost French scientists. Even in Paris his religious convictions emerged, when Cauchy, the celebrated mathematician, tried to convert him to Catholicism. The thing which baffled Cauchy was that Thomson's faith was so personal — he believed he *knew* his God.

Thomson was only twenty-two when the opportunity came for him to apply for the post of 'Professor of Natural Philosophy' at his father's university. In the face of stiff competition he was unanimously elected to become the youngest professor Glasgow University had ever appointed. Once again his religious convictions became apparent. In those days whenever a new professor was installed into office he had to publicly subscribe to the classic summary of Christian teaching, *The Westminster Confession of Faith*. So often this was done merely for the sake of tradition, but William Thomson went out of his way to impress upon all his deep commitment to those great articles of belief. It was this faith that sustained him when his father, who had been so close to him, fell victim to the terrible Glasgow cholera epidemic of 1848.

Every morning of the university term the young professor would enter his lecture room, mount the rostrum and repeat slowly and sincerely, eyes closed, a prayer for God's help, and this preceded every first morning lecture throughout his academic life.

Thomson had been professor just four years when he asked the university authorities for a room to use as a laboratory. At first they were quite taken aback, there being no such thing as university laboratories at that time. But to humour the young professor they gave him a disused wine cellar in a musty basement. It was not the last room they were to give him. In the space of a few years they would probably have given him the boardroom had he asked for it. For in that gloomy cellar — the first British university physics laboratory — the notion of modern academic research was born. Helped by thirty or so volunteer students Thomson cleared out the debris, cleaned the three small pavement-level windows and turned that room into a 'spearhead into the unknown'. The university soon gave him an additional 'think room' in the Tower, where some of his finest ideas came to him.

As a lecturer Thomson was evidently extremely difficult to keep up with. His lecture rooms were crammed full of apparatus, an unusual thing at the time. He followed no syllabus and he used no notes. 'Books?' he would retort, 'I am here to tell you what is not in the books.' He would speak in sudden bursts, always smiling. But suddenly an idea would occur to him and, giving the class an impossible-to-follow résumé of his idea, he would proceed to work out the underlying mathematics on a blackboard. The students, whether they understood or not, would watch 'a great scientist attack an unsolved problem...they saw him try one mathematical method after another in his attempt to wrest the secret from nature.'

His lecture room experiments became famous, particularly the one in which he calculated the velocity of a bullet. This made use of a heavy block of wood suspended from a metal frame by a swinging iron rod. As the rod swung it drew a tape measure out of its container. Thomson would take his rusty old rifle, adjust his eyeglass, take careful aim from a standing position and fire. As the bullet buried itself in the block of wood a great cheer would go up.

But Thomson had no equal fame for his explanations. One student wrote the following quotation in his notebook: 'The principle of the gyrostat is perfectly simple. It is merely a matter of generation of moment of momentum perpendicular to the axis of the rotator.'

As life turned out Thomson was to follow the role of his late father in more ways than one. He married a delicate girl of 22, endued with a deep faith and poetic gifts. But following an illness during their honeymoon she became a lifelong invalid. With touching care the professor looked after her, sitting through many nights of suffering with her. Small wonder he was pained by immature students who dismissed religion and scorned God with such self-assurance. His own faith had been tested in the fires of experience since childhood.

The constantly recurring problems of the Atlantic submarine-cable project were the means of Professor Thomson's sudden rise to popular fame. He was thirty when he was called in to help solve some of the seemingly insurmountable difficulties. 2,500 miles of cable were being laid by a British battleship and an American frigate, but the cable kept snapping and the whole expedition was wasting months on futile fresh attempts.

Thomson's first contribution was the invention of stranded high-conductivity cables. But his second great contribution was even more important. Once the cable was laid the signal transmitted at one end became so weak by the time it reached the other end as to be barely discernible. And after a very short operating time the cable would fail to yield any signal

The 'Great Eastern' on Atlantic cable duty

at all. The professor designed a galvanometer to record and amplify the tiny signal, and so made the whole practice of submarine-cable telegraphy a practical proposition. The most successful attempts at cable laying were carried out under Thomson's direction from Brunel's first iron-hulled vessel, the *Great Eastern*, a venture that earned a knighthood from Queen Victoria.

Sir William, as he then was, had reached his late forties when, not long after the death of his invalid wife, he was asked to write a series of magazine articles on the ship's compass. The first article appeared, but that was all, for as the great innovator wrote, ideas for its improvement flooded into his mind. Before long, the drawings of a completely redesigned compass reached the Patent Office. The new compass incorporated an entirely new approach. Unlike the traditional instrument, it did not stick, nor did it jump wildly to make reading impossible. Furthermore, to achieve total accuracy it took into account a ship's own magnetism.

The naval admiral who tested it described it as the first compass to really point north! In addition, Sir William had given it a better system for taking bearings to establish the exact position of a vessel. Not surprisingly this compass became the standard instrument for the Royal Navy. A yacht-owner himself, Sir William also produced a new invention for sounding depths, and another for determining the arrival of heavy seas, both of which became essential equipment to mariners. By the time he was fifty, his numerous inventions had already earned him a fortune. His official professor's house in Glasgow was the first home to have electric light (106 bulbs!) and he presented his old college (Peterhouse, Cambridge) with the first electric light installation to be seen in a university.

Still, however, the most prominent thing in Sir William's personal life was his faith. People knew him as an earnest churchgoer who never missed a Sunday at worship. They knew him as a supporter of Christian societies, particularly the National Bible Society of Scotland, and they knew him as a frequent speaker at Christian meetings. They knew quite well what he stood for, as the comment of a non-religious scientific writer shows so well: 'I would say he was a sincere Christian — meaning by Christianity that religion taught by Christ rather than the religion taught by the churches.'

Sir William's faith was certainly not merely a formal, 'respectable' acceptance of anything religious. He believed that God was to be found only by the route He Himself had revealed in the Bible. Deviation from the Bible was absolutely out of the question to him, for in his judgement any such deviation presented the people with a worthless, counterfeit religion. 'Priestcraft' and ritual he particularly shunned. 'All well-wishers of England and of religion in England,' he once said, 'must lament that there has been so much perversion allowed to go unchecked within the Church of England with only too feeble remonstrance on the part of the bishops.'

His later years were greatly helped by his devoted second wife, and he spent an increasing amount of time at a country house at Largs, where his best friend was the Free Church of Scotland minister, Dr Watson. A brief glimpse of the eminent professor in his sixties comes to us from the diary of his sister whose daughter Margaret married Ramsay MacDonald, leading to an interesting friendship between the ageing scientist and the rising politician.

Once when visiting his sister's London home, Sir William found himself housebound on the Sunday, the rain pouring down outside, and so he led the family in a Bible study. Later in the day his sister read out Darwin's statement of disbelief in divine revelation and the evidence of creative design in the universe. Sir William unhesitatingly rejected those views as unscientific. Earlier in his career he had calculated that the maximum possible age of the earth was 100 million years, a time far too short for the evolutionary process to have occurred. This led to a

Lord Kelvin with his ship's compass

long controversy with Darwin's advocate Thomas Huxley.

Almost inevitably Sir William was made a peer in recognition of his services to science, education and industry — taking the title 'Baron Kelvin of Largs'.

Naturally he had an enormous amount in common with Faraday, and so one of the most moving occasions of his life was when he was invited to unveil a memorial tablet to Faraday in London. How could he help telling the great company of assembled scientists and businessmen about Faraday's faith? The event occurred when the National Telephone Company installed their main London switchroom centre in the very building where Faraday had preached as an elder of a simple evangelical assembly. Speaking with great emotion, Lord Kelvin said:

'These walls tell a story, not of a magnificent cathedral, but of the humble meeting house of earnest Christian men. I well remember at meetings of the British Association in Aberdeen and Glasgow how Faraday sought out the meetings of his denomination and spent as a preacher or worshipper there the Sunday and any additional time he could spare. How very interesting it is to think of Faraday's lifelong faithfulness to his religious denomination.'

Lord Kelvin visited America many times, making a great impression on academic circles there. It is not generally known that he was the first man to perceive the enormous potential of the Niagara Falls for hydroelectric power, and it was his scheme which, eleven years after he designed it, became the first power station there. It was his powerful advocacy that accelerated the acceptance of Bell's telephone invention in Britain along with many other innovations from America.

By the time of his death in 1907, Lord Kelvin had to his credit over 60 published scientific papers, 70 patented inventions, and 21 honorary degrees. He had also received the Order of Merit and been made a Companion of Honour. Few scientists ever won public esteem as he did. From remarkable teenage brilliance and through 54 years as Professor of Natural Philosophy at Glasgow, his intellectual output had been immense. Though many of his inventions now belong to a bygone age, much of his theoretical work still serves as the basis of modern scientific understanding. Indeed, it was Lord Kelvin who first adopted the concept of 'energy'. *The Biographical Dictionary of Scientists* (London, 1984) comments — 'Kelvin was one of the greatest physicists of the nineteenth century. His pioneering work on heat consolidated thermodynamics and his understanding of electricity and magnetism paved the way for the explanation of the electromagnetic field later achieved by Maxwell.'

Throughout his life those around him loved his modesty and friendliness, and it was universally recognised that he was a man who had humbled himself under the rule of the Bible. He cleaved to the Bible as the only authoritative source of information about the *soul*, and would take time to explain it, with warmth and sympathy, to all who came into his circle of influence. Lord Kelvin truly considered himself purchased and owned by His Saviour.

The Prodigal Poet
James Montgomery

THE GREAT INFLUENCES which fashioned the life of James Montgomery — journalist and poet — stemmed from a 'profound change' experienced by his father as a twenty-year-old farm labourer working in the fields of Antrim. The field-preacher John Cennick had come to Ireland attracting large crowds at his services. Montgomery's father was one of many 'moved into anxiety about his sins and by and by finding pardon and peace at the feet of Jesus'.

Not long after joining a branch of John Cennick's Moravian church at Antrim, he married, and with his bride committed himself to serve as a Moravian missionary. James Montgomery, their first son, was born in 1771, soon after they went to minister on the west coast of Scotland, and when he was six years old he was taken to Fulneck, Leeds, where the Moravians ran a fine boarding school on a large farm.

Here, at Fulneck, surrounded by rough moorland and exposed to biting winds, Montgomery was given the combination of ultra-spartan training and warm Christian education in which the school excelled. Soon he was joined by his two younger brothers, for their parents were to sail for a term as missionaries in

Montgomery's birthplace, Irvine, Scotland

the West Indies. The happiness which the brothers knew at Fulneck despite the strenuous training and intensive teaching is evident from their many letters in adult life. 'I steal a few days once a year to visit Fulneck where I was educated,' writes James, ' — the dearest place to me on earth.'

It was a happiness flowing from personal experience of a walk with the Saviour, which was urged upon all the boys. 'There is no faith,' he reflected, 'for a young, warm, feeling heart like the evangelical faith. I believed; I enjoyed its blessings; I was happy!' While at school Montgomery found himself almost continuously writing verse, and beginning to dream of being a great poet. However, as an earnest young disciple he would hold his thoughts in check, remembering the words of the school litany: 'Keep us, our dear Lord and God, from untimely projects, from all loss of our glory in Thee.'

By the time he was sixteen he persuaded the school authorities to let him take a job, and they found him employment and lodging with a Moravian baker in the village of Mirfield. But before long his restless imagination and longings for 'action' plunged him into a near frenzy of frustration. One Sunday he wrote a highly apologetic note to his employer, collected together his poems, and set off with the vague idea of heading for London.

'I was such a fool as to run away with just the clothes on my back, a single change of underwear, and three shillings and sixpence in my pocket. I had just got a new suit, but as I had only been a short time with my master I did not think my service had earned it so I left wearing my old one.'

After two days of walking he stumbled wearily into a country inn south of Doncaster, where he was befriended by the teenage son of a nearby village shopkeeper. The shop was short of help and Montgomery was soon busy earning his living behind a counter once again. However, his fertile mind was still elsewhere — grappling with verse, and restless to move on into the unknown future. He had worked in that village more than three years when the shock news came that his mother had died from fever in the West Indies.

Young Montgomery had closely followed the work of his parents in their two consecutive pioneer mission stations. There had been five long years in Barbados during which the response had been cruelly disheartening. Then his father had written, 'I think the time of visitation appears to be at hand — we can no longer preach indoors, our regular listeners having greatly increased. Several of our baptised negroes began to tell others what God had done for their souls.'

Barbados had been followed by the planting of a new station in Tobago where no missionary had previously laboured. But here the fervent couple tirelessly preached and visited hut after hut in vain. 'Oh that I knew but one soul in Tobago truly concerned for his salvation, how should I rejoice,' exclaimed Montgomery's father in a letter. He had no sooner sent that letter, when his wife was taken ill, dying within a few days, but feeling 'certain that I shall be with Christ always'.

'She is at rest,' wrote the sorrowing missionary. 'May the Lord our Saviour comfort me. He is my only refuge and I confess, to His praise, I feel His presence and peace in an abundant degree.'

Less than a year later young Montgomery learned that his father had also fallen to the island fever and crossed the threshold of eternity. He felt as though a great responsibility had descended on his shoulders. He felt as never before a heavy sense of privilege. 'I am the son of missionaries. My father and mother laid down their lives in a far country in the service of the King of kings!' No matter how far he was to wander in future years from the faith of his boyhood, this strange sense of spiritual privilege and calling never ceased to humble and caution him.

Innocently glancing down the columns of *The Sheffield Register* one morning, Montgomery caught sight of an advertisement for a clerk in the town. He was nearing twenty-one, and felt it might be the change he wanted. Never did he realise that inside two years this 'clerk' would be thrust into the storm-centre of political controversy. The appointment would have been more accurately described as 'Personal Assistant to Joseph Gales, Editor of *The Sheffield Register*; Bookseller, Printer and Auctioneer'. Montgomery was appointed and given rooms at the firm's main office.

At that time the French Revolution had reached its most dramatic point, and political opinion in Britain had polarised for or against radical reform at home. Montgomery was expected to make a vigorous contribution to the *Register's* controversial opinions. 'At the height of this great argument I was led into the thickest of the conflict with all the enthusiasm of youth.' Caught up in the bustling programme of popular journalism and tract publishing, applauded by some, sneered at by others, and frequently flattered by his employer, Montgomery's head began to turn.

The provocative way in which *The Sheffield Register* advocated parliamentary reform was bound to invite reprisals from the authorities sooner or later. Inevitably the paper's editor committed the technical offence which the authorities were waiting for. He was duly accused of seditious libel, but fled the country before the arresting officer arrived. Montgomery at twenty-three was offered the finance to take over the entire business, and did so. The paper changed its format and continued publication under a new name — the *Sheffield Iris*.

The youthful journalist now had busy editorial schedules to keep, a political campaign to maintain, and a small but complex business to run. Tragically, the pressures and allurements combined to draw him

James Montgomery

more deeply into the world of politics, and away from his spiritual moorings. His principal friends were now antagonistic to biblical Christianity, and he hardly ever attended a church or chapel. Though he continued to write quantities of poetry, his work now became decidedly non-religious, much of it being written for the theatre.

Montgomery was caught out with disastrous consequences when he was asked if his printer could reprint an old ballad for a 'song-seller'. A mere 150 copies were printed at no profit just to keep the customer happy. But no one in the print shop noticed that the 'innocent' old ballad contained lines which — since the beginning of the war with France — had assumed an anti-patriotic meaning:–

> *For should France be subdued*
> *Europe's liberty ends;*
> *If she triumphs,*
> *The world will be free.*

The unfortunate publisher was speedily arrested. 'I am accused,' he wrote, 'of having wickedly, maliciously and seditiously attempted to overturn the King and constitution by force of arms — using what? — a halfpenny song!'

At Doncaster Quarter Sessions an eminent bench of justices duly assembled. After the prosecution had been conducted at great length followed by an hour and a half's speech from the defence counsel, the Chairman of the bench told the jury to find the accused guilty. Montgomery was sentenced to three months in York Castle prison.

Having completed the term it was not long before he was in trouble again. He reported in the *Sheffield Iris* how a Colonel of Volunteers had ordered a

The office of the 'Sheffield Iris'

Sheffield crowd, mainly composed of women, to disperse. When the people became defiant he rode into them slashing with his sword at women and children. Then he ordered the reading of the Riot Act, and bullets were fired into the crowd, several people being killed. The account of this event carried in the *Sheffield Iris* was clearly hostile to the Colonel, and Montgomery was inevitably prosecuted. In court the testimony of witnesses injured by the Colonel's sword was discounted, and the young editor went back to York Castle prison for six months.

In York Castle he stubbornly refused to join the meetings of a band of dissenting believers imprisoned for their refusal to pay parish tithes. He was already finding that 'the world is vain' but was not ready to return to the faith of his youth. Out of York Castle again, he wrote to his younger brother (who stayed on as a minister-cum-schoolmaster at Fulneck School) admitting that he suffered terribly from depression. 'I am seldom, so very seldom cheerful.' He carried within him 'a wounded spirit' and knew it. 'I have suffered much... there are three springs of continual unrest perpetually flowing within me: the cares of life; ambition for fame; and worst of all — religious horrors.

'Such has been my experience in the morning of life that I can never, never entirely reject it. What can I do? I am tossed to and fro on a sea of doubts and perplexities. The further I am carried from that shore where once I was happily moored, the weaker grow my hopes of ever reaching another where I may anchor in safety. At the same time my hopes of returning to the harbour I have left are diminishing. This is the state of my mind.'

The backsliding poet wrote so wistfully one winter evening:–

> There is a winter in my soul,
> The winter of despair;
> O when shall spring its rage control?
> When shall the snowdrop blossom there?
> Cold gleams of comfort sometimes dart
> A dawn of glory on my heart.
> But quickly pass away:
> Thus Northern-lights the gloom adorn,
> And give the promise of a morn
> That never turns to day.

After about seven years of trying to feed his soul on fame, influence, and worldly pleasure, Montgomery, approaching thirty, entered even greater depths of despondency. 'It is hard,' he wrote in a letter, 'to renounce the world and all those pleasures which the world deems innocent. Yet Christianity requires the sacrifice of them. For my own part I cannot at present take up my cross and follow the despised and rejected Man of Sorrows. And yet — you will say it is a strange confession — I carry a heavier cross and bear a deeper shame in my own self-rebuking conscience. I feel the Christian's suffering without the Christian's hope.

'My mind is not deeply laden with crimes but with unbelief; an unbelief from which I cannot deliver myself hangs heavy on my heart and outweighs all those petty joys for which I am unwilling to relinquish the world.' Strangely, this agonising period of indecision — longing for the lost experience of youth to return, yet reluctant to forsake the world — prevailed for several years.

The fall of Switzerland brought from Montgomery's ever active pen a remarkable epic poem, 'The Wanderer of Switzerland', which soared to instant success. Thousands of copies of the book were sold with the result that the poet's name became a household word overnight. Nevertheless, he felt no great elation or satisfaction, because the spiritual battle raging in his heart suddenly became all the more intense. Through the persuasion of his brother he began to attend services at a small Wesleyan chapel. Here he was extremely moved by a sermon by an eminent visiting preacher, Dr Adam Clarke. Later, he was to be quite overcome by the message of another visitor — William Carey — the pioneer Baptist missionary in India. The two men kept up a regular correspondence from that time. Yet he still could not bring himself to resolve the dilemma of his soul.

To his brother he confided: 'My heart aches so often that it hardly knows any other sensations than those of remorse, apprehension and despondency. We seldom seriously turn over our thought to eternity till we have been disgusted with the vanity and sickened with the disappointment of time.'

At the age of thirty-five, Montgomery really began to seek for the peace he had lost. One Sunday, having returned from a chapel service, he sat down with a book of sermons by the preacher who had been the means of his father's conversion. 'I took up a volume of Cennick's most simple but truly evangelical sermons and opened to one on *1 Timothy 1.15: This is a faithful saying, and worthy of all acceptation, that Christ Jesus came into the world to save sinners; of whom I am chief.* I read it over most eagerly and was very much moved and comforted by it.'

By now Montgomery was longing wistfully for forgiveness of all his sins, including that of unbelief and wilfully leaving the Lord. He ached for a renewal of the very definite spiritual experience of his youth, when the Lord heard and answered his prayers, and when he possessed so much evidence of the goodness and power of God towards him. His desires were reflected in his decision to stop attending and writing for the theatre. He even wrote publicly in a leading national magazine expressing his sorrow at ever having used Scripture flippantly or lightly in his poems. It was at this time that he wrote a hymn which includes the following verses:

> *I left the God of truth and light:*
> *I left the God Who gave me breath,*
> *To wander in the wilds of night,*
> *And perish in the snares of death.*

Sweet was His service, and His yoke
Was light and easy to be borne;
Through all His bands of love I broke.
And cast away His gifts with scorn.

Lo, through the gloom of guilty fears,
My faith discerns a dawn of grace;
The Sun of Righteousness appears
In Jesus' reconciling face.

'Never shall I forget the pleasure I felt in chapel meetings, with some of the poorest of Christ's flock. They were the only persons who cared for my soul. A change took place in my spiritual character from that time.'

While he had not yet fully recovered the peace and certainty he desired, his seeking now became more positive. Nevertheless, his public fame — which was increasing steadily as further poetic successes were published — somehow robbed him of the capacity to finally yield his life to Christ. Having been for seven years sick of the world, but unwilling to return to God, Montgomery now spent another eight years yearning to return, but never doing so.

'I am in the Spirit on the Lord's Day and I behold scenes of past happiness returning like lovely dreams upon me. I am transported back to the morning of life — the Sun of Righteousness is rising with healing in His wings. Alas! how long it is since I saw that Sun except in memory's melancholy eye! Why have I not already decided my condition for eternity? Is there anything more mysterious than that a man shall be dreadfully convinced of sin and yet have no confidence in God's mercy?'

I stir the ashes of my mind
And here and there a sparkle find.
Yet burns a fire within my breast,
Which cannot quench, and will not rest.
O for a gale of heavenly breath
To quicken life again from death!

An elderly Moravian minister wrote to him saying, 'How I shall rejoice to hear that the horizon of your soul is unclouded; that doubts have ceased to agitate your seeking mind; and that you have fully found again that unseen but ever-present Friend Who was the comfort of your early days. Convinced I was a sinner and stood in need of a Saviour I flew to Jesus, simply and childlike. O my friend, do the same, and there you will find rest for your weary soul.'

Then, at last, the time came when he found himself able to simply fall before Christ as the aged pastor had urged him to do. Laden with a sense of his rebellious, self-willed past, his pride and ambition, he trusted that his Saviour of old would receive him back and restore him. He longed to once again belong to Christ utterly and only. His faith and trust in Christ began to grow and flourish once again and at forty-three, for the first time in 26 years, trembling with anticipation, he approached the Table of the Lord in a Sheffield chapel, to take part in the Lord's Supper as a professing Christian. He had returned to the Shepherd and Guardian of his soul.

From that time on James Montgomery gave practically all his free time to evangelistic and particularly missionary support. Sunday afternoons found him with a class of young children in the Sheffield Red Hill Sunday School, and his pen became fertile in the writing of Christian hymns. Small wonder one of his

Medallion cast in Sheffield
celebrating Montgomery's eightieth birthday

own great favourites as a returned backslider was the
hymn of Toplady's containing the verses:–

> *The work which His goodness began,*
> *The arm of His strength will complete;*
> *His promise is Yea and Amen,*
> *And never was forfeited yet.*
>
> *Things future, nor things that are now,*
> *Nor all things below or above,*
> *Can make Him His purpose forgo,*
> *Or sever my soul from His love.*

In his day, Montgomery was a famous literary figure. His geographical writings were standard works; his poetic volumes were best sellers, and his numerous articles in the leading British magazines were highly acclaimed. From his mid-fifties he received various high public honours for his service to literature. Indeed, his publishers owed him such a debt of gratitude that they commissioned two leading men of letters to write an eight-volume memorial biography after his death.

After his return to the Christian faith James Montgomery wrote over 400 hymns, of which more than 100 are still in use today. Among the best known of these are: *Angels from the realms of glory; Stand up and bless the Lord; Command Thy blessing from above; Hail to the Lord's Anointed; O Spirit of the living God; Prayer is the soul's sincere desire.*

For the remainder of his long life until his death at eighty-three, Montgomery became conspicuous for his heavy involvement with 'ragged schools' (along with other benevolent enterprises), Bible translation societies and overseas missions. These last forty years of his life were — he would emphatically say — the happiest and the best of all, for he *knew* again the Lord and Friend of his youth, and *felt* His blessing, guidance and presence day by day.

Pioneer of Power
Sir John Ambrose Fleming

SIR JOHN AMBROSE FLEMING's life spanned some of the greatest discoveries of physics and electrical engineering. Not only did he have a direct influence on many of these discoveries, but he was the outright inventor of a number of key innovations including, in 1904, the radio valve, which made possible the development of radio and television technology, and remained *the* vital component of radio circuits for almost half a century. For this breakthrough, Fleming has been called the father of *modern* electronics.

John Ambrose Fleming was born into a 'parsonage'. His father held the degree of Doctor of Divinity and pastored a large, independent congregation at Kentish Town, London. In those days Kentish Town was a well-off suburb on the edge of green fields stretching up to Highgate and Holloway. Fleming was eleven when he witnessed a very moving period in the life of his father's church. This was in 1859, the year when a great spiritual re-awakening took place in England. In the space of a few months the pastor's son saw hundreds of new people coming into the church, listening with great earnestness to the message preached, confessing their sins in prayer to God, and going on to experience the full meaning of Christian conversion. While we cannot say when Fleming experienced conversion for himself, he professed to know Jesus as His Lord by the time he was a young man.

Fleming did not have an easy passage to success in his chosen field of study — science. He was sixteen when he started studying for a science degree at University College, London. The Bachelor of Science degree at that time included Mathematics, Chemistry, Physics, Botany, Zoology, Geology, Physiology and Mental Philosophy. Fleming's father could not afford to keep him at university, so he had to do most of his study privately while earning his living as a stock exchange clerk. Despite this handicap he was one of only two students to attain First Class honours in his degree.

Being keen to teach, at twenty-one Fleming became the science master of a public school near Blackpool. However, his restless mind soon led him back to London for further studies at the Royal College of Chemistry. When his savings ran out, he was compelled to return to teaching, this time at a Cheltenham school. But after three years he finally decided that a schoolmaster's life was not for him. He longed to go to Cambridge and secure a degree that would open the way to a research career, but as his savings were not enough to see him through he needed to win one of the very rare scholarships offered in those days.

Once Fleming formed an aim there was no holding him, and by October 1877 he had won such a scholarship and entered St John's College, Cambridge. While there, he studied under Clerk Maxwell and found considerable opportunity to exercise his shrewd, penetrating mind with research work,

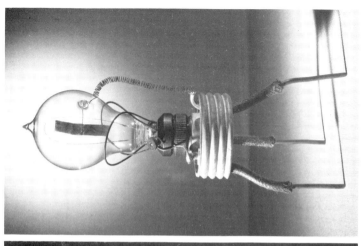

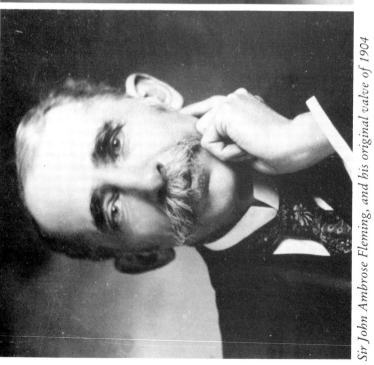

Sir John Ambrose Fleming, and his original valve of 1904

earning the Doctor of Science degree. No sooner had he left Cambridge, than he was appointed a professor at University College, Nottingham.

Fleming's industrial fame started at the age of thirty-two, when he was called in to advise the newly-formed Edison Telephone Company, and to act as a key scientific witness in their famous legal battle with the Post Office. When the Bell and Edison telephone companies merged, it was Professor Fleming who designed many of their early exchanges.

Numerous inventors had tried for years to make an electric light for domestic use, but no one had succeeded. Then J. W. Swan of Newcastle made a glass bulb containing a thin filament made of a carbon rod. When connected to a supply of electricity, the carbon rod became white-hot. Swan improved his lamp by making the filament out of toughened cotton coated with carbon. This bulb gave the light of sixteen candles! Hot on Swan's heels came the energetic inventor Edison, who went a step further than Swan. He decided to provide towns with an electricity supply to work the new bulbs, and in 1882 he appointed Dr Ambrose Fleming as his company's Chief Electrician.

Electric lighting was initially laughed at by the gas industry which thought it posed no threat whatsoever to gas lighting. Fleming put the first electric light system into a British ship, the HMS Mooltan. At the same time he could see that a system of standardising electrical instruments was urgently needed, and his strong pleas led to the Institute of Electrical Engineers pressing the Board of Trade to set up a laboratory to achieve this. It is now known as the National Physical Laboratory of the United Kingdom.

The alternating current method of generating and

distributing electricity was born outside Britain, but it
proved to be a sick child. It was Fleming who cradled
the invention, giving it life and credibility. At the
South Kensington Inventors Exhibition of 1885, a
Hungarian inventor demonstrated a machine called an
alternator. It was driven by a steam engine, and
generated electricity in such a way that the flow of
current changed direction in the wire fifty times every
second.

The inventor had discovered that this 'alternating
current' could be stepped up to a very high voltage by
transformers, enabling the current to travel great
distances without loss of power.

An engineer named de Ferranti carried these ideas
further in England. He persuaded a group of wealthy,
titled people to sponsor a scheme to set up a power
station at Deptford to produce a high voltage supply
capable of providing power to the whole of the West
End of London. De Ferranti built gigantic alternators
and transformers to make electricity at 10,000 volts,
but whenever the system was turned on, the switch-
boards caught fire and cables burned out. It just
would not work.

Professor Fleming was called in to solve the problem. He found that de Ferranti had no means of
overcoming the problem created when blazing arcs of
electricity extending up to several feet in length
jumped across the switching gear. Fleming discerned a
way of eliminating this effect by redesigning the
system, and the Deptford AC power station became
a going concern. Needless to say he was soon asked
to design electricity supply schemes for Exeter,
Taunton, Peterborough and Plymouth.

The contribution to science which Fleming made
went far beyond these industrial feats. At the age of

The Prince and Princess of Wales visit the Poldhu transmitter in 1903

thirty-six he became the Professor of Electrical Engineering at University College, London, a position
which enabled him to govern the training and research
of future electrical scientists for four remarkable
decades. Professor J. T. MacGregor-Morris says in the
Dictionary of National Biography, 'His forty-one
years of service to electrical engineering (as professor)
coincided with a rapid growth in the subject, and he
was one of the small number of English scientists who
contributed greatly to its progress.'

Busy though he was in scientific affairs, Fleming
had another loyalty, a loyalty to the Friend he had
found as a young man. He began to be less quiet as a
Christian believer, and to use his remarkable powers
as a lecturer in speaking about the Bible. He loved the
Bible, and studied it as the Word of God. 'It contains,'
he said, 'records of events quite out of line with
normal human experience, and predictions — some of
which have been already remarkably fulfilled. Though
written by the pens of men, there is abundant
evidence that it is not the product of the human mind.
By countless multitudes it is, and always has been,
revered as a communication to us from the Creator of
the universe, the supreme and everlasting God.'

At the turn of the century Professor Fleming took
on one of his most important pieces of consultancy
work. He became advisor to the Marconi Wireless
Telegraph Company. Marconi was the young Italian
inventor who first made a wireless telegraphy system
work. Naturally, his invention captured the public
imagination, especially when he decided he would try
to 'bridge the Atlantic' by radio. He called in Professor Fleming, who realised at once that Marconi's
wireless apparatus was much too small. Fleming
designed a massive piece of radio equipment — trans-

forming Marconi's ideas to the size of an engineering plant.

He sited it down in Cornwall at Poldhu Point, high on a cliff facing out to the Atlantic. A twenty-five horsepower engine powered an alternator which gave 2,000 volts. Huge transformers raised this to 20,000 volts. Marconi designed the aerials and in November 1907 he left Professor Fleming and his assistants at Poldhu, from where they would transmit a signal, and he set out for Newfoundland to receive it. There, he set up his receiver, fed by huge aerials hung from balloons and kites.

On 12th December, 1907, Marconi and his friends heard in their earphones a faint morse code signal for the letter 'S', sent out from Cornwall. Radio waves had crossed the 'mountain of land covered by sea', which was Fleming's definition of the Atlantic. The progress of radio telegraphy had been propelled forward by the essential technical expertise of Fleming, and in particular by his best-known invention, the radio valve, without which it would not have been feasible. Marconi devised the principle of long-distance radio transmission, but Fleming made it work.

The radio valve owed its birth to Fleming's curiosity over unexplained phenomena observed in the course of his researches. Many years before he had noticed a peculiar thing about Edison light bulbs. Whenever those old-fashioned bulbs became overheated, the inside of the glass became blackened, except for a thin line which remained clean and clear. Fleming half-realised the cause of this, and consequently spent a great deal of time studying the phenomenon in his laboratory. It led him to invent a device derived from a bulb which would serve as a

An early Fleming valve of 1905

'one way street' to an electric current. Electricity could flow through the device in one direction but not in the other.

It was not until he started advising Marconi on wireless, that Fleming realised that his 'one-way' device, or 'valve' as he called it (because it was the electrical equivalent of the one-way valve fitted in water supply pipes), was the vital missing part to the progress of radio technology. He patented it in 1904, and it became known as the Fleming radio valve or diode (and later — 'the two-electrode thermionic rectifier'). It was the forerunner of hundreds of different kinds of valve essential to all radio and electronic equipment for fifty years.

Although now superseded by transistors, valves made possible the phenomenal advance in radio and television technology which, in time, gave birth to the transistor. Fleming's triumph was undoubtedly *the* great milestone in electronic engineering this century. The valve itself, however, should not be thought of as obsolete. Much highly specialised electronic equipment still depends on sophisticated types of valve. Moreover, the principles employed in the household television tube as well as in the ubiquitous VDU originated with Fleming's brilliant invention of 1904.

By 1929, Professor Fleming had been honoured with a knighthood, umpteen distinguished medals from learned societies, and numerous honorary fellowships and degrees. On four occasions he was invited to give the Christmas Lectures at the Royal Institution, because few others could equal his skill in enthralling an audience. He was an exceptional speaker for getting complex scientific concepts across to non-scientific audiences, and was constantly invited to lecture in crowded halls all over the country. Sir John's career was also exceptional in the enormous contribution he made to scientific writing. Copies of his published works kept in University College, London, fill five volumes.

It would have been an easy and comfortable course for John Ambrose Fleming to hold his peace over the theory of evolution. The scientific tide then ran in its favour, and anyone who disagreed ran the risk of

Part of the original Poldhu transmitter

ridicule. But he could not bear to look on quietly while something that he *knew* to be unproven and unscientific was blatantly taught as a fact to the general public. In 1904, the same year that he patented the radio valve, he launched a vigorous personal campaign to put the 'other side', beginning with a major public lecture which was published and sold in large numbers under the title, *The Evidence of Things Not Seen*. He became a great supporter, and for a time the President, of a notable society formed for scientists and other academics who wished to raise their voices against the spurious reasoning of the theory of evolution. This was the Victoria Institute. One of Sir John's papers on the subject of population growth and the age of the earth demonstrates the impossibility of the human race being as old as the evolutionists imagine. It represents one of many lines of argument pursued by Sir John and other outstanding thinkers in his circle.

As one of the greatest engineers and scientists of his time, Sir John played a major part in almost every significant electrical invention and project over a period of nearly fifty years. He retired in 1929, the year that saw the launch of another invention that owed its existence to the radio valve — Baird's first television. Sir John Ambrose Fleming, however, never really retired. To the closing years of his long life he maintained his involvement with the electrical sciences, serving as President of the Television Society, and advising a new generation of researchers. He read his last scientific paper to a learned society at the age of ninety!

However, in 'retirement' he was able to devote much more of his time to speaking on public platforms to draw men and women to the authority and message of the Bible, and to the Saviour Whom he knew and loved. Sir John crossed the borders of eternity to meet his Lord in 1945, his inquisitive mind looking forward to a realm of infinite wonder, of which the greatest marvels of this present world are but a token.

Island of Despair
Daniel Defoe

London was in the midst of wild celebrations. Bonfires lit up the night skies and thanksgiving torches burned merrily in ground-floor windows. People danced and laughed and drank toasts on the open streets until the gutters literally ran with ale. But there were no celebrations in one tall, narrow house in Cripplegate. Here, on this warm May evening of 1660, James Foe, a tallow chandler and a staunch Puritan, stood at his window brooding sadly over fickle London. As he saw it, the acclamation was not for Charles II and the restoration of the crown. It was the farewell party to high moral standards; a joyous shout of welcome to a monarch who would usher in pleasure, vanity, drunkenness and licentiousness.

In the small living room behind the tallow shop Mrs Foe sat in her heavy oak chair nursing the latest arrival to the family — named Daniel, but not christened because his parents had Baptist convictions. It was a hard time to be born into a nonconformist family. Mr Foe's pessimism while the rest of London celebrated was to be amply justified. Within two years of Charles II's coronation, nonconformists were enduring cruel persecution.

First there was the Great Ejection, when the Foe's local parson — Dr Annersley of St Giles — and 2,000 other clergymen were ejected from their churches. Their crime was their refusal to bow to odious new practices imposed on the church by the high-churchmen now in control, practices calculated to drive out Bible-loving clergy. The expelled preachers left the Church of England on what became known as Black Bartholomew's Day, 1662, never to return.

Like many others Dr Annersley built a nonconformist chapel and his entire congregation joined him there. But the arm of persecution soon reached out again when it was made a crime for nonconformists to hold any kind of service anywhere. A single magistrate was given the power to send offenders to prison, or even to deport them for seven years. Preachers were dealt with particularly severely, John Bunyan's twelve-year imprisonment being one among many cruel sentences imposed at that time. Ejected ministers were forbidden to work, live or even visit relatives within five miles of their old parishes.

Stamped indelibly on Daniel's memory as a little child, was the awful insecurity of Sunday worship. When darkness fell, Mr and Mrs Foe would slip out watchfully with their three children and make their way to a small hall where the steadfast Dr Annersley continued to tend his flock.

Daniel Defoe (he assumed the different form of his name as a young man) was a wide-eyed five-year-old when an invisible terror stalked the streets of London. The Plague brought agonising death to 100,000 Londoners, about half the population, and sent tens of thousands fleeing into the countryside. Carried by armies of rats living in the rubbish-strewn narrow streets and rotting timber houses, the Plague of

London reached its height at the Cripplegate area.

Years later Defoe was to become its major chronicler in his magnificent work, *Journal of the Plague Year*. But at the time, as a frightened child, he peered daily out of the small window of his 'room beneath the thatch' to see scores of people leaving town with their possessions piled high on carts. He could see vacated homes with large red crosses painted on their doors, and the words 'Lord have mercy upon us'. Late in the evening, as he lay awake in bed, he would hear the grinding sound of cartwheels straining under some heavy load. A handbell rang — a dull, metallic, empty sound; and a hoarse voice called, 'Bring out your dead!'

The Foe family 'migrated' to their upper floor and cut themselves off from the outside world to pass unscathed through the period of plague. But before very long they were to witness another major catastrophe — the Great Fire of London — which began in Pudding Lane and went on to destroy the whole of inner London in three terrible days. Daniel Defoe never forgot the faces of horror-struck adults gazing helplessly at the wall of fire which had engulfed their homes and worldly goods, nor the relief of his own household when the fire stopped just short of their home. He remembered how Dr Annersley preached with extraordinary power and passion in a great open-air service held amidst charred and smouldering ruins.

Just a few years later young Defoe was regularly to be found seated in Dr Annersley's study, hundreds of venerable, leather-bound books looking down at him. There, under individual tuition, he was thoroughly grounded in English and maths. The old doctor deeply impressed him. He was a gentle man, so warm and kindly. Yet he was also a very firm man, possessing courage which kept him resolutely at his ministry throughout the nonconformist persecutions.

However, it was the next stage of Defoe's education which did most to furnish his effervescent mind with the material it needed for the future years. At thirteen years of age he was sent to the Dissenters' Academy at Newington Green, London. The Academy was a rambling and rather decrepit mansion, but in these old-fashioned surroundings boys received an education way ahead of the times. Classics mattered little. Instead they were subjected to highly compressed courses in law, science, geography, astronomy and shorthand! After these came logic, maths and modern languages, and every student had to learn to make a long speech without notes, and to master the art of verbal argument. Interestingly enough, the boys also had a say in the running of the school, all discipline being in the hands of a school parliament made up entirely of pupils. Equally interesting is the fact that the boys themselves hated this 'democratic discipline', most of them feeling that it led to a lax and immature school.

Already Defoe was growing into an extreme activist. A strongly-built young man with dark eyes and a bulldog-like jaw, he quickly assumed the prime role in his student circle. Not only was he the acknowledged leader at the academy, but among the young people in the Cripplegate area he was also invariably at the hub of any unusual activity. But Defoe could see a world of difference between his friends in the academy and Dr Annersley's congregation, and those 'outside'. He believed in God. He believed that it was possible to know God personally, and he was absolutely convinced of the power and reality of personal faith in the lives of his parents and many of his church friends. Yet the strange thing was that somehow Daniel Defoe, as a young man, never seems to have yielded his own life to the Saviour he knew so much about. Always he looked at the faith and lives of others. Always he was impressed, convinced, filled with respect — but always he remained a stranger to the experience of conversion, and to a walk with the living God.

Mr and Mrs Foe earnestly hoped that their son would become a minister, but he was far more interested in commerce. So, on leaving the academy he became a merchant's apprentice. It quickly became evident to his employers that Defoe was no ordinary apprentice, and he was promoted to serve the firm as a representative. Then, with a few years' experience behind him, he joined a company of commercial travellers touring Portugal, France and Italy trading for British firms.

Back at home, aged twenty-three, he decided to become his own master. In Cornhill, London, a new business opened under the large painted sign, 'Daniel Foe, Merchant'. The money for this came mainly from his newly-wedded wife Mary, a deeply religious girl whose wealthy father had given her thousands of pounds on her wedding day. Defoe, while keeping up a good, nonconformist churchgoing manner, now threw himself into the things he counted of most value. How he loved trade! Not the small-time shop-keeping of his father, but high-risk overseas buying and selling. It was a fortune he was after.

Also, it was an age of bright, utopian projects coming one after another from the pens of progressive writers. Defoe, with his love for argument and ideas, leapt into the arena and began to publish his own schemes and formulae for ending all the problems of the world. Gradually, he became a well-known figure in all the upper-class clubs of London. His great preoccupation was quite simply — the promotion of himself. The flamboyant men's fashions of that time afforded ample scope for vanity, and Defoe became a master of expensive clothing. Giving little time and attention to his growing family he enjoyed riding his superior black stallion to places where he could mingle with the titled gentry, looking every inch a rich courtier.

Defoe seems to have taken every possible oppor-tunity to get away from his devoted wife, attending all the provincial trade fairs whether he needed to or not. He had only been married two years when he rode down to the West Country to enlist in the army of Monmouth. With the death of Charles II the crown was about to pass to James II, a passionate Catholic. Monmouth, the Protestant rival contender for the throne was Defoe's political hero. But after a brief skirmish Monmouth was captured and arrested. Defoe escaped unscathed, but very shaken, and made his way back to London. When savage sentences were imposed on Monmouth's supporters, he kept quietly at his merchant's business, hoping against hope that no one in London would hear of his involvement in the affair.

As his courage returned, Defoe resumed his activity in the growing political movement which opposed James. He even founded a nonconformist house church, taking pastoral oversight himself for two years. But the novelty of this soon wore off. It was little more than a passing effort to win God's favour by exercising the head knowledge of Christian things learned in his youth. His interest was next transferred to the study of history, because to write political pamphlets for vast distribution one needed to know the historical background to everything.

It did not take a writer with Defoe's ambition and talent long to grip the public imagination. Taking advantage of the mounting popular feeling against the king, his words found a ready audience in the clubs, coffee houses and streets of London. So he argued, pleaded and fumed as one of the major Whig pamphlet writers. Then, at long last, the day every Protestant and Whig had been longing for arrived. On November 4th 1688, William of Orange landed at Torbay to take the power of discredited King James.

Defoe's Stoke Newington house

As for Defoe, success now seemed to be following him in every way. Acknowledged as principal pamphleteer for a popular cause; increasingly acclaimed for his published poetry; applauded wherever he went to make public speeches; and now beginning to make some quite startling gains in his business affairs, he was riding the crest of a wave. But then, with cruel suddenness, catastrophe overwhelmed him. First, a few heavy and unexpected trade losses severely shook his finances. Then, due to the war with France, two merchant ships heavily laden with his merchandise failed to arrive at their destination. Morning after morning Defoe went to the London Post Wharf, nerves taut, face drawn, hoping for good news. If these vessels were lost, he would be ruined. Eventually word came. They had fallen into enemy hands. One of the proudest men in London was reduced at a stroke to the position of a bankrupt fugitive.

Bankruptcy in those days met with heavy penalties — punishments which Defoe had no intention of suffering. Making hurried arrangements for his neglected family and putting all his property into the hands of his most pressing creditors, he went into hiding. Fortunately for him his wife, aided by a loyal friend, arranged a settlement for him which gave him a chance to have another try with his business, provided that his debts were made his first priority. But the terrible blot of bankruptcy had clearly wrecked all his ambitions for political position and honour; his enemies would see to that. Still, the incorrigible spirit of Defoe was soon pursuing again an ambitious course of self-advancement. Putting pen to paper he wrote a book solving a few more of the world's problems, advocating relief measures for oppressed businessmen and suggesting higher education for women. Queen Mary happened to read it and approved of his ideas very warmly. It led to an audience, and yet another audience, and from that time Defoe became a regular visitor at Court. Now he was all the more determined to put his financial failure into the past and restore his tarnished image. The slight change of name to the more aristocratic-sounding Defoe was contrived at this time for the benefit of the king and queen.

He particularly impressed William of Orange as a man of ideas, and when the royal fortunes were low it was largely Defoe's proposal that led to the setting up of large-scale royal lotteries. Twice he was principal trustee of these nationwide draws which offered people an immense prize for a tiny stake.

Another of Defoe's shrewd ideas to pay off magnificently was his scheme to build a brick factory at Tilbury. At that time Britain imported practically all her bricks and tiles, so the home product, baked from clay dredged from the estuary, was an unknown quantity. But it sold very well, forming the masonry of some of London's largest buildings and inspiring the emergence of a new British industry. Free from debt and rich once again, Defoe was entirely caught up in high life and pleasure. He became noted for clothes, carriages and royal connections.

To avoid the reproaches of his anxious, unhappy wife he spent most nights out in West End taverns. His six children — two boys and four girls — grew up virtually fatherless when Defoe, following the promiscuous ways of fashionable society, took a mistress at Tilbury. In due course his mistress gave birth to a son, a child who was to carry and suffer all the blemishes of his father's character and know nothing of his successes.

For the present there seemed no pang of conscience, no personal shame, no kind of setback or disappointment which could shake the vanity, ambition and money-worship of this brilliant young man. No qualms troubled him even when he sat down to write pious pamphlets about religious abuses, such as when he attacked the practice of some nonconformists who attended Anglican communion once a week to qualify for civil service posts. 'An upright man has only one religion,' he wrote, 'and he dare not play hide and seek with the Almighty.' At the age of thirty he was regarded as one of the greatest writers of his time.

So the years flew; years of profanity; years in which his children grew into adolescents who despised their fame-crazed father; years in which pamphlets and poems streamed from his pen. The best-selling poem for nearly a century was Defoe's answer to people who criticised William of Orange as a 'foreign prince'. Entitled *The Trueborn Englishman*, it light-heartedly traced the descent of the English from historic invaders to form the most mongrel race in the world. It became so popular that almost everyone could quote it.

William and Defoe had become very firm friends. Indeed, Defoe was one of the sovereign's closest confidants. He gave regular advice on the political climate, acting as a kind of agent with special responsibility for watching the movements of William's political opponents. When new ministers of state were being considered, Defoe would tell William who among the nominees was safe and loyal. Famous, rich and in the confidence of the king, Defoe's haughty manner and position had gained him many enemies in high places. Suddenly, with the premature death of William, he found himself exposed to them — a hated and vulnerable man. Newgate Prison lay ready. His enemies waited their opportunity.

William's early death changed many things. His pro-Catholic opponents celebrated enthusiastically, for the successor to the throne was to be Queen Anne, the pro-Catholic daughter of James II. The queen was a cowardly woman who used cunning and deceit rather than face criticism for making open decisions. In no time she had gathered around her ministers of state opposed to the old administration. Defoe's future prospects were not only at a low ebb but he stood in grave danger of victimisation by the new anti-Whig, anti-Protestant ministers who had too often smarted under the whiplash of his pen. Their moment of revenge came very soon.

Certain high-churchmen had made efforts to get severe punishments enforced for nonconformists.

Queen Anne

Defoe, who was a staunch (if nominal) supporter of nonconformists, anonymously wrote a pamphlet called 'The Shortest Way with Dissenters'. It was calculated to turn public sympathy in favour of nonconformists by urging the most extreme measures against them in a highly arrogant tone. 'Pull up this heretical weed of sedition,' wrote Defoe, tongue in cheek. 'If one severe law were made that whoever was found at a conventicle [a nonconformist service] should be banished from the nation, and the preacher hanged, we should soon see an end to the tale.'

To Defoe's alarm the pamphlet failed to arouse the sympathy of the public for nonconformists. In fact, the reverse took place. Many people took it seriously and agreed with it! One well-known clergyman wrote, 'Next to the Holy Bible and the Sacred Comments, I take it for the most valuable piece I have.' Nonconformists were horrified, and so furious was the ensuing argument that Defoe rushed out an explanation, revealing that he was the writer.

This was just what his enemies were waiting for. Without hesitation the Earl of Nottingham, Home Secretary, ruled that the pamphlet had ridiculed the clergy and caused a breach of the peace. Defoe must be arrested immediately. Terrified, he fled into hiding, knowing only too well that Nottingham was in a position to ruin him at one stroke. He would have him thrown into Newgate Prison for 'high crimes and misdemeanours', where he would spend the rest of his active life in degradation with the 'scum of all society'. Once there, his tile factory, source of a lucrative income, would be bound to fail within a few weeks of his absence, leaving his wife and family penniless. He would doubtless contract prison disease and die a wretched, early death.

Every day that went by he heard that more officers had been put on the search for him. Frantically he wrote a long plea for mercy to Nottingham offering to do anything — even raise and lead a cavalry troop — rather than stand trial. But Nottingham wanted his man. He planned to strip him of everything and have him publicly humiliated. 'He is a middle-sized man,' ran the 'wanted' description, 'about forty years old, of a brown complexion and with dark brown hair. Wears a wig, has a hooked nose, a sharp chin, grey eyes, and a large mole near his mouth.'

Within a matter of weeks a despairing Defoe was successfully hunted down and committed to Newgate. It was a nightmare to him — the circumstances and the people connected with these events never leaving his mind. In later years his novels teemed with passages inspired by his Newgate experiences. But worse was to come. Lulled into a false sense of security by his legal advisers Defoe pleaded guilty at his trial. Having been led to believe he would be fined and released, he was crushed beyond imagination when the judge sentenced him to three sessions in the public pillory and a life sentence. The day after his trial he lay trembling on a rough wooden bed in a dark, stone cell feeling life had come to an end. Then, suddenly, a way of escape came to his mind. For a moment he was stunned that it had not occurred to him before. A resurgence of self-confidence and optimism swept through his body as he leapt from his bed to seize pen and paper.

It was well known that Defoe had acted as a political agent for William of Orange. In that task he had made it his business to know all the sordid secrets and cunning intrigues of the leading politicians. If some of those secrets were now to be 'leaked' many significant people would be in very dangerous predicaments. So Defoe wrote to a high official offering to tell the queen all he knew. It had the effect he planned. Anxious politicians began to panic. To the surprise of the callous Newgate warders, Defoe began to have

numerous eminent visitors. Naturally they brought
their friendly good wishes and asked after his health.
But they all had another matter they wished to raise.
If he would keep his mouth firmly shut they would
undertake to protect him from the pillory and try to
secure his release.

He dreaded the prospect of the pillory for it was
a spectacle which drew out the worst instincts of
the common people of London. They particularly
relished the fall of a 'toff' or 'dandy', and came armed
with rotten eggs, bad meat and horse dung to enliven
their depraved entertainment. To offset their rancour,
Defoe wrote a hilarious popular poem about the
pillory which was printed and circulated the day
before his session.

When the officers led him out of Newgate an
unprecedented unofficial escort waited outside. Numerous politicians with their footmen and hired men
stood ready to flank the procession to the pillory.
Once there, they formed a dense protective wall
around him. The reaction of the crowd was quite
unexpected. Softened by Defoe's comedy pamphlet
and struck by the novelty of a guard around the
pillory they felt a strong regard for the victim. For
hours he was treated like a celebrity. People crowded
to look, just as they might clamour to see the influen-
tial and famous, and for the first time ever, flowers
were thrown instead of the usual offensive missiles. It
had never happened in London before. Defoe went
out to be pilloried, and returned to Newgate an
idolised man.

At this stage a new influence entered Defoe's complicated life — that of Robert Harley, the ambitious
Speaker of the House of Commons and undoubtedly
the shrewdest tactical politician of the day. Harley,

who became Queen Anne's favourite and who was later made Earl of Oxford, had been watching Defoe for some time. At first he disliked his boastfulness, but gradually he came to see the potential value of his versatile pen. Defoe, he decided, would work for him. Harley sent money to relieve Mrs Defoe's financial difficulties and set about getting Defoe pardoned. Within five months he was a free man — or so he thought. It would be much more accurate to say he was now Harley's man, and he soon learned what Harley expected of him.

He was to be the sole editor of a new, twice-weekly paper called *The Review*, the object of which was to promote Harley and his party. Harley would be its owner and director, though secretly of course. In Defoe's hands *The Review* rapidly became the best-looking and largest circulating paper of the day. For nine years it not only moulded public opinion but set completely new trends in journalistic reporting and presentation. It was this journal that secured for Defoe in later centuries the accolade — the father of modern journalism. Tirelessly he poured out news and comment, increasing publication to three times weekly and extending the circulation throughout the land.

As far as his personal life was concerned Defoe remained firmly gripped by the love of wealth, pomp and fame. The humbling effects of Newgate had been short-lived and he was now as remote from his wife and children as ever he had been. Years flew with Defoe at the hub of the turbulent world of politics. Harley lost power, changed parties, and within two years was installed by Queen Anne as Chancellor of the Exchequer (at that time the 'Prime Minister'). Defoe, of course, was obliged to swallow his pride

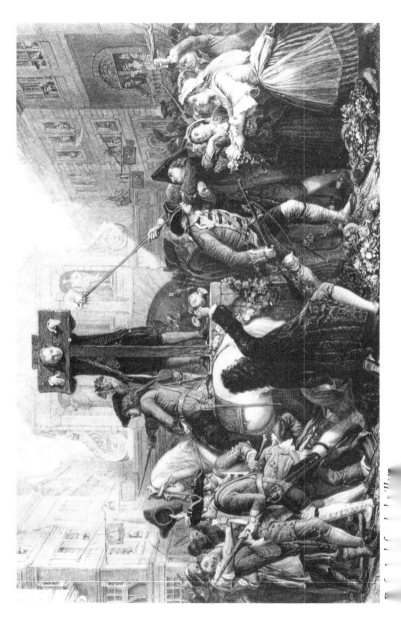

and switch policies with his master, losing many of his personal friends in the process.

Those who were jealous of Defoe's journalistic success, together with political enemies who wanted to see an end to the paper, now circulated malicious rumours about his past financial failure. At the same time his tremendous work-load and dissipated life-style began to take its toll upon his health. Defoe realised that he had given the years of his prime to a paper which now ruled his life, and he felt the deep-seated despair of a man who has found that the world is vain. He had invested in wealth and fame, to reap only toil, jealousy, hatred, heartache, and failing health.

At this point a series of bitter blows struck hard and deep at his remaining self-confidence. The law in those days put all writers — especially controversial ones — in a very vulnerable position. His enemies found grounds to have him brought before the courts once again for publishing seditious matter. Probably he would have been acquitted, but in the heat of the moment he passed comments about the honesty of the judge who was due to hear his case, and the Lord Chief Justice intervened personally to commit him to prison for contempt of court. Harley came to the rescue and secured his release, but within a year Defoe was facing fresh charges. Although these were never pressed, the damage was done: the scandal of these arrests broke the link with Harley, now Lord Oxford, and the newspaper work finally came to an end.

Defoe was almost a spent man, looking much older than his fifty-four years, when his reflections on life at last drifted from self-pity to a realisation of his own failure. This new-found humility and self-examination began to germinate during a serious illness which confined him to bed for several weeks. All he could do was allow his thoughts to range across the painful ups and downs of his life. The ache of thwarted ambition gave way to a throbbing remorse that he had so shamelessly sacrificed his family for personal success. One after another the wilful deviations from his Christian upbringing rose up before him to accuse him, and gradually a change took place in his whole life and outlook.

It was a change all the more remarkable when it is remembered that Defoe had travelled extensively, moved in both the lowest and highest circles, known imprisonment and very great affluence, and had both absorbed and influenced all the culture and politics of his period. He had done all the things he had ever wanted to do, and suffered all the things he had wanted to avoid. Yet for all this, the most profound influence·in his life came to him at fifty-five years of age while confined to a bedroom. It was a change which transformed him from a leading political journalist to a man whose pen became devoted to writing books with a moral and spiritual message.

Defoe described his personal conversion to Christ most graphically in his best-known novel *Robinson Crusoe*, for Crusoe's religious experience was nothing other than Defoe's spiritual autobiography. Crusoe had been for some time on the barren island which he called the 'island of despair'. Having lost all sense of danger, he busied himself with ingenious and industrious ways of building his own empire.

'But now,' he says, 'when I began to be sick, conscience, that had slept so long, began to awake, and I began to reproach myself with my past life... Then I cried out, "Lord, be my help for I am in great distress." This was the first prayer, if I might call it so, that I had made for many years.

'My conscience presently checked me ... and methought it spoke to me like a voice: "Wretch! Look back upon a misspent life!" I took up the Bible and began to read ... the first words that occurred to me were these: *Call on me in the day of trouble, and I will deliver, and thou shalt glorify me.* ... Before I lay down, I did what I never had done in all my life, I kneeled down and prayed to God to fulfil the promise to me, that if I called upon Him in the day of trouble, He would deliver me.'

Four days later Crusoe found himself very much recovered. 'I took the Bible, and beginning at the New Testament, I began seriously to read it ... but I found my heart more deeply and sincerely affected with the wickedness of my past life ... I was earnestly begging of God to give me repentance, when ... I came to these words, *He is exalted a Prince and a Saviour, to give repentance and to give remission, [referring to the Lord Jesus Christ, Who died on the cross to take the punishment of sin, and is therefore able to forgive sin].*

'I threw down the book, and with my heart as well as my hands lifted up to Heaven, in a kind of ecstasy of joy, I cried out aloud, "Jesus, Thou Son of David, Jesus, Thou exalted Prince and Saviour, give me repentance!" This was the first time that I could say, in the true sense of the words, that I prayed in all my life; for I now prayed with a sense of my condition ... Now I looked back upon my past life with such horror, and my sins appeared so dreadful, that my soul sought nothing of God but deliverance from the load of guilt that bore down.'

Following more earnest prayers Crusoe felt and knew great comfort within, sensing that God had forgiven him. He then began spending time each day reading his Bible and praying. Three months later he recorded: 'I gave humble and hearty thanks that God had been pleased to . . . make up to me the deficiencies of my solitary state by His presence and the communication of His grace to my soul — supporting, comforting, and encouraging me to depend upon His providence here, and hope for His eternal presence hereafter. I began to feel how much more happy this life I now led was . . . my very desires altered.'

Crusoe's words described exactly Defoe's own case. He tasted and felt the nearness of the Saviour to him, answers to his prayers, and a great change in his own inner character. Indeed, all his tastes and inclinations were altered by the touch of God upon his life, so that he became in every sense a new person. In Crusoe, Defoe portrayed not only his own experience, but that of countless millions who through history have known the dramatic nature of true conversion to Christ.

In the novel, Crusoe is made to record these words two years after his conversion: 'I looked now upon the world as a thing remote, which I had nothing to do with, no expectation from, and indeed no desires about.' And so it was for Defoe also. The grip of the world over him, its glamour, pride and selfish pleasure, was now broken. Its powerful allurements were now cheap and hollow in his estimation. A new value-system reigned within — a hunger and thirst for better, deeper things.

Defoe made rapid progress in his walk with God because he had been well taught in his childhood by sincere, believing parents. All the knowledge of the Bible and of the Lord so long covered up by the years took on new relevance. Soon his pen was at work drawing a picture of what his own family life should have been. He wrote as one who mourned deeply because his own family had grown up without a father who really loved them and cared for them spiritually. His words extended to a book which was published under the title *The Family Instructor* and which broke all sales records. King George I read it regularly to his children.

His tongue went to work in personal witness — explaining to others the change which had taken place in his life. The spiritual conversation of Robinson Crusoe and Man Friday gives a vivid picture of what it was like for Defoe when he began to speak to others about Christ.

The idea for the novel *Robinson Crusoe* came from the experience of real-life sailor Alexander Selkirk, who had been marooned on an island for four years. Defoe wrote an introductory paragraph and passed it to a friendly publisher, who commissioned the book. It is a solid indication of Defoe's fertile imagination and capacity for work that the entire book was completed inside four months. The haste with which it was written gave rise to the well-known contradictions in the book. Indeed, it is believed that Defoe never even read it through. But the gripping quality of the work made it an instant success, and set an entirely new standard for all future narrative literature.

A number of further novels followed. *The Life, Adventure and Piracies of the Famous Captain Singleton* was another best seller which also had a conversion message written into it. *The Misfortunes of the Famous Moll Flanders* was the harrowing story of a girl who experienced just about every possible vice and misfortune, ending in repentance and conversion — in the original novel.

The Remarkable Life of Colonel Jack and *The Fortunate Mistress* also had underlying religious themes. It is a significant tribute to Defoe's powers that all these early eighteenth-century titles continue to be in print and available today. They teem and swarm with plots and sub-plots reflecting the breadth and versatility of Defoe's remarkable imagination. Not surprisingly many have regarded him not only as the father of modern journalism, but also as the true father of the modern novel.

For fifteen years Defoe strove to be as active as possible in Christian work, conscious of his wasted past, and yet believing that God would fulfil a promise made in the Bible, *I will restore to you the years that the locust hath eaten.* And the Lord did bless his later years, so much so that subsequent generations were to associate his name with the books which bore a testimony to the converting power of the Saviour. The once vain social climber had become a humble, genuine and warm person, concerned for the eternal souls of those around him.

At the very end of his life he was plunged once again beneath the shadows he had known for so many years. At the time of his bankruptcy years earlier, a business friend had paid his debts on the understanding that he would repay with interest. This he had done, but neither he nor the friend had kept receipts. When the businessman sold his interests to others, his records showed Defoe as still owing the money. Twenty-six years later a woman who inherited these interests sued for the whole sum.

Defoe had no legally acceptable evidence for his defence. Aged seventy he faced the possibility of bankruptcy all over again. Appointing his eldest son to look after his affairs, the distraught old man went into hiding to think things out, visited only by his wife and daughters. He took refuge in a simple lodging house in Ropemaker's Alley, in the City of London, just a stone's throw from the place of his birth. Here, on the night of April 26th 1731, he went to sleep for the last time. Perhaps the sadness and trouble returned at the very end to remind him of the vanity and cruelty of the world, by contrast with what lay ahead for him, for by the morning he had left his 'island of despair' for ever and arrived on the eternal shore to be with his Saviour.